WHAT MATTERS AND WHO MATTERS TO YOUNG PEOPLE LEAVING CARE

A New Approach to Planning

Peter Appleton

T0278451

First published in Great Britain in 2024 by

Policy Press, an imprint of
Bristol University Press
University of Bristol
1–9 Old Park Hill
Bristol
BS2 8BB
UK
t: +44 (0)117 374 6645
e: bup-info@bristol.ac.uk

Details of international sales and distribution partners are available at
policy.bristoluniversitypress.co.uk

British Library Cataloguing in Publication Data
A catalogue record for this book is available from the British Library

ISBN 978-1-4473-6833-5 paperback
ISBN 978-1-4473-6834-2 OA ePub
ISBN 978-1-4473-6835-9 OA PDF

Cover design: Nicky Borowiec

Contents

List of boxes

About the author

Peter Appleton read psychology, zoology, and philosophy at Durham University before training as a clinical psychologist at Glasgow University and doing further postgraduate studies at Strathclyde University. During mid-career he completed a PhD in behavioural epidemiology at Liverpool University Department of Public Health and Policy. He worked for 32 years as a clinical psychologist in multidisciplinary Paediatric and Child and Adolescent Mental Health teams in Oxford, Norwich, North Wales, Cambridge, Bedford, and Peterborough (Youth Offending Service).

In parallel he held academic posts at Bangor, Cambridge, and Essex universities, conducting research in the areas of self-concept and paediatric neurodisability (spina bifida), the role of social support in smoking cessation in pregnancy, and care coordination in services for children with a disability.

Recently, at the University of Essex, he has conducted (with colleagues) two qualitative research studies with young adults in transition from out-of-home care, including a study funded by the Economic and Social Research Council (ESRC) Impact Acceleration Account at Essex University. This book builds on these studies.

He edited *Children's Anxiety: A Contextual Approach* (Routledge, 2008) and has published, with interdisciplinary colleagues, in journals such as *Qualitative Social Work, Journal of Pediatric Psychology, Developmental Medicine and Child Neurology, British Journal of Health Psychology*, and *British Educational Research Journal*.

He is currently Visiting Fellow at the School of Health and Social Care, University of Essex, UK.

Acknowledgements

My deepest thanks go to the participants and staff in the London and Suffolk services where the research studies which led to this book took place, and to my research colleagues Dr Isabelle Hung and Dr Caroline Barratt. Caroline Barratt and Peter Appleton acknowledge with sincere thanks a grant from the ESRC through the University of Essex Impact Acceleration Account (grant number ES/M500537/1) for the Suffolk study.

Thanks to Professor Margaret Archer for a key meeting at Warwick University in May 2009, and very helpful subsequent correspondence.

Thanks to Miriam Richardson, systemic psychotherapist, social worker, and friend, for discussion on systemic theory, extended discussions on Margaret Archer's theoretical work, and learning about Miriam's work with unaccompanied and asylum-seeking young people. Miriam was a critical friend both before and throughout the whole time of developing the ideas in this book.

A Zoom call with Emily Munro at an early stage in formulating this book was of very significant help – thank you. Thanks to the organisers (Emily Munro, John Pinkerton, Mike Stein) of the Leaving Care Research Workshop held at the Institute of Education in London in September 2014, for an invitation to present data from our first study of internal conversations. Feedback and discussions at this meeting were formative for the development of our work. Thank you to the International Research Network on Transitions to Adulthood from Care for the opportunities to network with colleagues across the world.

I am grateful to colleagues at the University of Essex for support and shared ideas over 12 years: Frances Blumenfeld, Danny Taggart, Susan McPherson, Victoria Joffe, Leanne Andrews, Chris Green, and Gill Green. Thanks to Katrine Sundsbø and Hannah Crago for help with Open Access. Without Frances Blumenfeld's leadership and support the research for this book would not have been possible – thank you Frances.

Thanks to Oskari Kuusela for the Wittgenstein seminars at the University of East Anglia.

During the writing of this book, my thanks to many colleagues: for copy-editing of the book proposal to Harriet Evans; to Caroline Barratt for thoughtful readings of early draft chapters; to Meri Kulmala of the University of Helsinki for discussions and her reading of several chapters of the book; to Pekka Mäkelä of the University of Helsinki for his reading of Chapter 8; to Natalie Glynn-Wix at the University of Tübingen for her reading of Chapter 1, and follow-up email exchanges. Thanks to Elaine Matchett of Coventry University for the opportunity to think together about planning in the contexts of care-leavers' journeys through further and higher education, and the opportunity to contribute to a joint paper.

At Bristol University Press I have been very fortunate to work with Isobel Bainton who has been a supportive and thoughtful editor. My thanks also to Jay Allan, Inga Boardman, Vicky Delahunty, Rich Kemp, Kathryn King, Colin Morgan, Susannah Sallé, Sophia Unger, Ruth Wallace. Four anonymous readers provided enormously helpful feedback at various stages. My thanks to Celine Parent for the index.

I remember with great warmth my colleagues in my first post-qualifying job, in the 1970s, at the Park Hospital for Children, Oxford, for their wonderful generosity, and for the day-to-day experience of genuine interdisciplinary work, within and between practice and research, and a first professional opportunity to learn about the impact of child maltreatment on children and families; to the memory also of May Davidson at the Warneford Hospital, my first boss; and to Oxford colleagues for the opportunity to see and hear Jerome Bruner presenting his ground-breaking research on the social bases of early language development. I am grateful to my colleagues at the Peterborough Youth Offending Team, in the late 2000s, for the opportunity to work collaboratively with a wide range of disciplines. And to the young people, who were always willing to talk, not always willing to see a psychologist, but from whom I learned so much. Many were in care, and some were about to transition from care. Thank you.

Thanks to Catherine Appleton for reading and commenting on material, key advice at various stages of publishing, and discussions about criminal justice aspects; to Ed Appleton for detailed comments and discussion on the whole manuscript, including social work aspects; to Hilary Appleton for loving support and dialogue throughout.

I am grateful to the Editor of *Qualitative Social Work* and to Sage Journals for their kind permission to use material published first in this journal. The papers are as follows:

Hung, I., and Appleton, P. (2016) 'To plan or not to plan: the internal conversations of young people leaving care', *Qualitative Social Work*, 15(1): 35–54.

Appleton, P. (2020) 'Anchors for deliberation and shared deliberation: understanding planning in young adults transitioning from out-of-home care', *Qualitative Social Work*, 19(5–6): 1130–1146.

Introduction

This book is about planning – but planning with a difference.

A conventional idea of planning might bring to mind goals and objectives – and 'future orientation'.[1]

But let us imagine that planning might also be thought about from a completely different perspective.

Let us imagine that at least for some young people who have had a seriously and repeatedly adverse upbringing, planning – as we usually think about it – may be an alien concept. Not only an alien concept, but if asked about how one thinks and feels about planning for the future, a young person might say: "I don't believe in it – I don't, I don't. I don't believe in it."[2]

The point of this book is to suggest that, for *some* young people, especially some of those who have experienced severe and compounded adversity, planning as we might usually think about it – goals, precise future plans – may not be a helpful 'starting point'.[3]

Building on work by philosopher Michael Bratman[4] – and others – this book takes as a core idea a *three-aspects* model of planning. Each aspect is richly detailed. One aspect concerns what is important – *what matters and who matters*: not a list, but a detailed personal account of what and who counts in each of our lives – for instance (imagine being a young adult leaving out-of-home care) an attachment to a foster parent who continues to help out, a concern about a birth parent who is struggling, some new housing accommodation that is a financial worry. A second aspect is *shared deliberation and shared planning* – meeting up with close friends (as one research participant said, "we've just been through it together ... we were like family"), deciding on accommodation with the help of a previous foster mother, getting a regular and reliable lift to college. And, finally, planning in relation to how we

1

think about time. Bratman refers to this as 'temporally extended intentional agency' – forward- and backward-looking – mental time travel – creating and managing plans in our own time. Inspired by some young people's deep scepticism about planning for the future, I re-imagine this third aspect to include alternative, queer,[5] crip,[6] and highly individual approaches to how past and future time are seen – *a sense of personal time*.

This flexible three-aspects model of thinking about planning may be especially relevant to young people who are in transition from out-of-home care, and busy trying to build a life. Crucially – and this cannot be emphasised too strongly – this open-ended and non-dogmatic model of planning may be especially relevant to care-experienced young people, not because of a supposed lack (or 'deficit') of future-oriented planning skills, but rather because having been in care *brings a rich hoard of experience to each of the three aspects of planning agency* – or so I argue in this book.

The rich hoard of experience usually includes very complex interpersonal losses, multiple emotion ruptures, and understandably 'unfinished business' or 'emotion-work-in-progress' linked to compounded adversity. A distinctive feature of this book is that, following Martha Nussbaum and others, we frame emotions as intelligent, as 'intelligent responses to the perception of value' and as 'suffused with intelligence and discernment'.[7] As 'intelligent responses to the perception of value' emotions are relevant to/ intertwined with planning, or so I suggest throughout this book, and in particular in Chapters 9 and 10.

There are four chapters at the heart of this book (Chapters 3–6) in which we listen carefully to what a diverse set of eight young people, all transitioning from care in London, England, have to say about planning – including what and who matters, their accounts of shared deliberation, and *their own highly individual approaches to time and planning*. The innovative research interview my colleagues and I conducted, designed by sociologist Margaret Archer[8] as part of her empirical and theoretical work on the interplay between agency and structure, was open-ended, semi-structured, and focused – crucially, at the beginning of the interview – on young people's self-reflective accounts of their own internal conversations.

Why internal conversations?

Origins of our research

This book grew out of qualitative research interviews held with a small and diverse sample of young adults (there were nine, aged 19 to 24) who were in the process of transitioning from out-of-home care (foster care, kinship care, or residential care) in London, England (Study 1: Hung and Appleton, 2016).[9] The focus of our research was on 'internal conversations' – those interior dialogues we have with ourselves – for instance mulling over, rehearsing, deciding, ruminating, *and* planning. Planning was only one item on our 'short list' of internal conversation interview prompts,[10] and was not, at this stage in our research, a major focus. We were interested in how young people used *all* their internal conversations to navigate and negotiate, psychologically and socially, through their own complex and often extremely stressful worlds of transition from out-of-home care.

(Transition from out-of-home care to an 'independent' life usually involves challenges finding accommodation, work, and further or higher education, often without the close family support many young people have, and against a stacked deck of structural inequality. The young person may be involved in trying to re-build relationships with birth parents – from whom she or he was removed earlier in life, usually because of abuse or neglect. The young person is also more likely than their peers to be experiencing mental health and drug misuse issues, and more likely to be involved with criminal justice systems, linked to multiple risk factors during childhood and adolescence. Some young people, despite being in care, will have been victims of criminal or sexual exploitation.[11])

In our London study of internal conversations in young adults in transition from care one finding stood out. It was that most of the young people said that they didn't plan for the future. They explained, often at fascinating length – and mostly with very strong emotion – that forward planning was a waste of time, and that, to quote one participant, "nothing goes to plan anyway".

Although there were just nine participants, the sample was heterogeneous. We 'purposively' included young people who were doing relatively 'well' – in work or education – through to those who were 'struggling' and/or NEET (not in education, employment, or training). The four women and five men varied also by ethnicity, number of family/residential placements, sexual orientation, and previous education. What was really striking was that *all* of the young people were sceptical about future planning.

At the time, we had no idea whether this finding might be true of a wider or more representative sample of young people transitioning from care in England, or indeed elsewhere.[12]

We knew that the community service we had recruited the nine participants from was well resourced, and that all the participants had engaged in formal/pathway/transition planning (since 2000 this has been a legal requirement in the UK[13]) and had been well supported by staff.

Indeed, when discussing 'planning', the young people were not usually talking about the formal transition planning process provided by the local authority. After 'drilling down' into the qualitative data – into the narrative accounts the young people gave us about their internal conversation worlds – we concluded that these young people were saying something more fundamental, or 'existential', about planning, and about how the future seemed.

A few years later, the opportunity arose to conduct a second study.[14] We used the same qualitative internal conversations interview[15] with a similar age-range sample, in a rural part of England. The participants were six young adults, aged 18 to 20, living in Suffolk, in the East of England: three NEET, two employed, and one in college. Again, we found a strongly expressed reluctance to plan for the future for *all* participants (Study 2: Barratt et al, 2020).

Summarising so far: from our two published qualitative studies in England there is a suggestion that 'thoughtful and expressive scepticism' about planning for the future is an important aspect of the experience of *some* young adults transitioning from out-of-home care.[16]

This finding was understandable, given the precarious and traumatic circumstances many had experienced during childhood and adolescence, and were experiencing during transition. Multiple traumas, long-term uncertainty, family and school disruption, and precarious access to work and housing are likely to undermine the young person's development of 'future orientation' and 'planning skills'.[17]

It is also understandable, given the precarious access to housing, work, and education that *many* young people experience, globally, in the early twenty-first century – not only those leaving care.[18]

And, in addition, emerging adulthood is regarded as an experimental time of life, with exploration of roles and commitments taking the psychological high ground, rather than concrete plans for the future.[19]

There are *many* reasons why some young people might be sceptical about planning for the future – although, we were focused on the specific reasons given by the young people in our studies who were in transition from care (Chapters 3–6 in this book).

But there was something else in the research interviews that helped us begin to think *radically* differently about planning – specifically for young people leaving care. We were struck by the young people's self-reflective and deeply thoughtful answers to the internal conversations interview question 'Which areas of your life matter most to you at the moment?'

The transcripts of even the young people who were 'struggling' the most, and whose internal conversations seemed, to use sociologist Margaret Archer's word, 'thinnest',[20] had a relatively rich and expressive narrative to share with us about which areas of their life mattered most to them at the moment. In this interview section there were thoughtful autobiographical accounts of what mattered most and who mattered most in the young people's lives. The question seemed to free up – or to 'quicken' – the young people's thinking.[21]

To take one example, for Corrina[22] (woman, aged 20) it was her family that mattered most. By family she meant both her foster family and her birth family. She had been estranged from her birth mother and father for some years. Recently her birth father had been in touch and wanted to meet up. She described the complex decision. It involved talking with trusted friends, and a great deal of internal dialogue, and she was helped in her decision by imagining what her deceased paternal grandfather might have advised – she had warm and loving memories of him.[23]

Corrina did not endorse *future* planning – either for the immediate day-to-day future or for the longer-term future – "No, not really 'cos it never goes to plan anyway".

But, if we take a step back, and think of planning differently, more broadly, and more flexibly, isn't there a sense in which the decision whether or not to see her birth father involved complex planning? The decision required her (rather suddenly) to 'dig deep' into her own thoughts and feelings about what mattered in her life, recall memories of her father and how he had treated her, imagine her much loved paternal grandfather's 'voice', talk with trusted friends about the decision, think about her emotionally complex relationships with other members of her birth family, and perhaps imagine, even for a moment, a future in which he, her father, would have a part.

In this one major decision, *all three aspects* of Bratman's 'remarkable trio' of planning[24] are evident – *what and who matters* is a deep and complex question for Corrina to address in this practical decision-making; in *sharing these deliberations*, she talks with others who are close to her, and imagines what her grandfather might have said; and, as far as *planning and time* are concerned, she weaves memories from the past with what is important for the present and in some sense thinks about the future, albeit rejecting the overall idea of future-oriented planning.

Why is this important?

Paraphrasing what one colleague said to me, these findings – even if they apply only to a small-to-moderate proportion of care-leavers[25] – are important because they challenge one of the assumptions some of us carry into our first consultations with clients, that is, that the client will have a goal or a plan or will at least want to have a conversation *about* a potential goal or a plan.

In leaving care services there are transition plans to be collaboratively considered.[26] In medical and nursing care there may be a treatment plan to discuss and then self-manage into the future.[27] In psychotherapy and mental health care, collaborative therapeutic goals and user involvement may be encouraged.[28] In education there are (future) assignments to be planned, scheduled, and completed (and before that, courses to be considered, applied for, and so on).[29] In juvenile justice and criminal justice services there may be a discussion about planning how to find work and accommodation, and avoid committing offences in the future, and, if incarcerated, a forward plan for release.[30] In substance misuse services there may be discussion about a client's 'patient-oriented' goals.[31]

Each of these 'contexts' is built around an assumption that the young person will: (a) wish to think about their own future, and (b) want to deliberate on how they might 'influence intentionally (their own) functioning and life circumstances', that is, exercise agency.[32]

In this book, our approach will be to allow our qualitative research findings – that some care-leavers actively *do not wish* to plan for the future – to challenge the assumption that clients will usually consider forward planning. Once we mull over this challenge to orthodoxy, other questions arise: why *would* we assume that clients wish to plan for the future? How did this idea come to be the norm, at least in certain cultures/societies? Is the idea that 'future orientation' is a 'strength' – among young people with a history of maltreatment[33] – a concept that can be supported without a psychosocial understanding of 'context' (structural inequality contexts, developmental and family experience, current circumstances, and broader psychological aspects of the individual)? Is our expectation that clients will wish to plan for the future – or can be helped to plan for the future – a hegemonic idea? And can we think differently, and more broadly, and especially more flexibly, about 'planning' and what we have come, in some cultures, to call 'goals'? And what exactly do we mean by *precise* goals? Precise in what sense? From whose point of view (these five words said slowly and expressively!)?

Purposes of the book

This book is concerned with beginning to think about planning differently, more broadly, and more flexibly, with a clear focus on young adults experiencing compounded adversity.

The aims of the book are:

1. To provide an in-depth discussion of planning agency in young adults in transition from out-of-home care, from a position of (a) respecting the detailed reflexive self-interpretations and 'voices' of young people themselves and (b) acceptance and

understanding that some young people do not wish to plan for the future.

2. To allow philosophy and theory of planning agency to interplay with young people's own narratives about internal conversations and planning agency.

3. To suggest cross-disciplinary practice implications via addressing a question in the final chapter: can young people's *own starting points* for planning also be the starting points of services, or potential services,[34] starting points for research and service co-design and co-production, and starting points for individual help and support? Each of these areas is by definition *planful* in some sense: but whose sense?

4. To take a philosophical ('epistemological') position on theory and on qualitative language-based data, based on (late) Wittgensteinian thinking,[35] this approach focuses, in practical terms, on how precisely we might, non-dogmatically, think and speak differently, more broadly, *and more flexibly* about planning under conditions of adversity. This philosophical position itself has (non-dogmatic) implications for practice and for research design.

The 'shape' of the book

What Matters and Who Matters to Young People Leaving Care: A New Approach to Planning is organised around the idea of beginning to think about planning differently, more broadly, and more flexibly, with a clear focus on young adults experiencing compounded adversity. At the heart of the book are four case-based chapters (Chapters 3–6) in which I report very detailed accounts of eight young people's (care-leavers') own thoughts and feelings about planning – to be precise their own thoughts and feelings about what and who matters most in their lives at the moment, and the personal and dynamic logic each individual young person brings to their thinking (and feeling) about planning, including planning for the future. Chapters 1 and 2 prepare the ground for the case-based chapters, introducing the ideas of internal conversations and reflexivity (that is, young people's reflexivity), and how we might think of reflexivity as making planning possible – in the real and deeply challenging world of leaving care. In Chapter 2 I expand the idea of reflexivity to include a fuller range of reflexivities: self-reflection, embodiment, shared deliberation and intersubjectivity, and mental time travel. These four rich human reflexivities are all strongly evident in the interviews with young people that I discuss in Chapters 3–6.

In Chapter 7, which interplays with Chapter 8, young people's rich and thoughtful narratives from Chapters 3–6 are summarised, and we see the initial shape of the provisional three-aspect approach to planning. First, I note the reflexive and expressive detail, via mental time travel, of individual care-leaver's accounts of *what matters and who matters*. Second, I consider the importance of the careful unpacking of subjective time in relation to planning – *a young person's own sense of personal time*. Third, I discuss how *shared deliberation and shared planning* – with friends, family, professionals – is for some young people a highly valued aspect of planning – even for young people who regard themselves as highly self-reliant. These three aspects (of planning) might each be viewed as a 'strength', in contrast to the view that a 'lack' of future-oriented planning might be regarded as a vulnerability.

Chapter 8, 'From reflexivities to planning: the "remarkable trio" of Michael Bratman', begins with a detailed account of Michael Bratman's model of planning agency (see earlier in the Introduction), followed by a reflection and reformulation of one aspect of Bratman's model – the cross-temporal aspect, based on the wide range of experience of time and planning discussed by young people in Chapters 3–6, as well as a wider literature on subjective time. Bratman's 'remarkable trio' interplays with young people's narratives summarised in Chapter 7 and the core idea for this book of a *three-aspects* model of planning. Finally, I outline what we might mean by individual, personal, dynamic, autobiographical, and highly expressive, *logics* for planning.

In Chapter 9, 'Emotions: a background framework is called into question', following Martha Nussbaum's work, I frame emotions as 'suffused with intelligence and discernment'; and we 'grapple with the messy material of grief and love, anger and fear',[36] and stretch our own senses of time by reminding ourselves that healing usually takes time, and that young people in transition from care may have much to teach us about *emotions, time, and planning*. I emphasise the circumstances of being in care and leaving care, which might involve multiple emotion ruptures, transition itself as a potential emotion rupture, particular experiential and hermeneutic aspects of transition, and emerging adulthood as an opportunity to make sense of, review, revise, reframe, rethink, consider new and renewed relationships, and plan – in the broadest and most flexible sense.

In Chapter 10, 'Planning and voice: starting points', I ask the question: can young people's *own starting points* for planning also be the starting points of services, or potential services,[37] starting points for research and service co-design and co-production, and starting points for individual help and support? Each of these areas is by definition *planful* in some sense: but whose sense? I begin with the poet and playwright Lemn Sissay's inspirational phrase 'flags in the mountainside'.[38] Second, I discuss recognition theory, a major source of contemporary thought – and debate – about voice, and the struggle for minoritised peoples to be heard. Third, I discuss participatory co-design, an approach to research and practice which provides an opportunity for young people's voices not only to be heard, but also to be included in actively defining the scope and form of a project. I discuss a wider literature on co-design and co-production, arguing that there is much to be gained from the cross-fertilisation of ideas. Fourth, as an example of cross-fertilisation across the wider expanses of the literature on co-design – in relation to the research reported in this book – I tentatively apply the notion of 'methodological sensitivities for co-producing knowledge through enduring trustful partnerships'[39] to the co-design of transition planning with young people in transition from out-of-home care.

1

Reflexivity, internal conversations, and the transition from out-of-home care

Preamble

As if we were listening to a piece of music – say jazz – that starts with a few sounds, and then plays with the sounds, reverses their order, shakes them all about, hands the idea over to a different instrumentalist, hears some 'atonal' variations that question orthodoxies, I want us to consider thinking about planning differently, more broadly, and more flexibly, with a clear focus on young people experiencing compounded adversity. The metaphor of jazz (and I understand that some readers will not be jazz fans) is multi-layered, with the origins of jazz in racism, oppression, discrimination, segregation, and with the extraordinary flowering of a different sort of music, a music that questions what music is.

Charelle, Danny, and their internal conversations

Charelle is a 20-year-old woman in transition from out-of-home care. She has spent 10 years in foster care, during which she was excluded from school, and subsequently left school at age 14. She has no educational qualifications; she is looking for work. She hopes to start a course soon.[1]

Early in a research interview about internal conversations (see Introduction for why and how we were interested in young people's internal conversations, and see Box 1.1 for details of the internal conversations research interview), Charelle gives an example:

'I'll replay situations in my head first – like I'll replay it as if it's happening again, like if that makes sense – scenes of what happened – and sometimes I'll rethink about what happened and how I should have changed that decision, if that makes sense. I don't know – I just use my brain [laughs].'

The research interviewer asks whether 'replay' happens for recent events or for more distant events. Charelle replies: "It depends … 'cos of the life I grew up in some things from my past affect what's happening now, so it depends. I have to rethink what happened then to help me decide what I'm gonna do now, if that makes sense?"

The research interviewer asks Charelle if she could give an example.

'Maybe when it came to moving out and living on my own for instance.[2] A lot of the things that happened in the past – I never grew up with my parents obviously, so I never had no one to teach me stuff and that, so it affected [me] obviously when I moved out and I had to make decisions: "Do I wanna move out – I don't know anything – do I move out and learn it all myself?" But then I had to rethink back to my past obviously because my past affected how I thought about things, because certain things still affect me from my past which still affect me now with my future, if that makes sense. Like my Dad came back into my life recently and obviously I had to think about all the past things that happened to decide if I want to be in contact with him.'

Charelle tells us a lot in this very short interview extract.

Box 1.1: The internal conversations interview framework

This qualitative interview framework was developed by Professor Margaret Archer, for general population and student population use.[3] We used it, after careful piloting, in two studies of young adults in transition from out-of-home care.[4]

The purpose of the face-to-face, semi-structured, open-ended, qualitative interview is to enable the participant to discuss their experience of internal conversations about the social world – their own 'mulling over' of their experience of day-to-day social life, including internal dialogue about past experiences, what matters most in their life at the moment, and plans for the future. It is by design autobiographical. 'Prompted' internal conversations include, for instance, deciding, imagining, and mulling over, but the interviewer is equally interested in idiosyncratic forms of internal conversation. The interviewer is also interested in the participant's self-reflections on their own patterns and styles of internal conversation.

As a qualitative interview the focus is on the meanings generated by the young person and the young person's account of how they came to have that particular way of seeing their social world. For instance, if a young person says that she frequently imagines what her deceased grandfather or grandmother might have said – about some current issue for the young person – the interviewer invites the participant to talk about how she came to develop this particular imaginative internal dialogue, and how it connects with everyday life in the present, as well as the past.

The internal conversations interview has two main sections. In our first study we conducted the interview in the form of two separate interviews, separated by a few weeks.[5]

Interview 1

The purpose of the first section – our first interview – is to enable the young person to discuss their experience of internal conversations. The interviewer emphasises that 'we are all different', and 'there are no right answers' – 'many people experience conversations with themselves, or self-talk, silently in their heads'; 'I'd like to know whether this is so for you and if you could tell me a bit about this experience?' Each participant is encouraged to discuss their internal conversations, in their own terms, for as long as they wish. Following any individual examples of internal conversations offered by the participant, the interviewer provides ten specific prompts (not necessarily in this order, and carefully referencing any individual types of internal conversation already raised by the participant): planning, rehearsing, mulling over, deciding, re-living, prioritising, imagining, clarifying, imaginary conversations, and budgeting.[6] Afterwards, participants are again asked whether they had found any other ways of doing internal conversations.

Interview 2

In the second section (our second interview,[7] a few weeks later) the researcher focuses on two main areas: what matters and forward planning.

First, the interviewer asks the question: 'Which areas of your life matter most to you at the moment?' The question allows the young person to discuss freely what matters or what and who is important in their life – entirely from their own perspective. In addition to the opportunity to talk freely and openly about what and who matters, the participant is also given the opportunity to discuss how long each 'matter' has been important, whether the matters 'dovetail' smoothly, whether or not time was spent thinking out exactly what they should do in the light of what mattered, and whether aspects of background experience had been helpful or unhelpful in the 'realising of concerns' (that is, taking forward any projects based on the personal formulation of what matters).

Second, after a participant has discussed their account of which areas of life matters most to them at the moment, they are encouraged to discuss any plans for the future. In the original interview framework,[8] the wording of this section includes 'life-projects', 'her own future', and a range of suggested subsequent questions about remuneration, repute and responsibility, sacrifices and regrets, ambitions, commitments, and re-orientations. In our collaborative pilot work with participants,[9] we quickly realised that this wording was unhelpful for the young people we were interviewing (and perhaps for many young people/emerging adults still forming their ideas about their futures). Most participants in our studies had already 'flagged up' during the first interview that they did not do future-oriented planning. We therefore modified the way we asked this key question, asking instead for further elaboration of their own particular thoughts and feelings *about* forward planning, and about planning in general. We conveyed an openness to the young person's *own position* on planning, time, and so on.

Let us take another example from a young man of the same age as Charelle.

Danny is a 20-year-old man. He had spent 3 years in residential care after a lengthy period of severe family instability. He had, like Charelle, left school at the age of 14, and had had no further formal education. He was employed in retail.

In the internal conversations interview, Danny[10] gives an example of how he experiences internal conversations:

> 'I actually do have conversations with my actual mind … it's like your consciousness … your mind tells you what you need to know, what you wanna hear and what you wanna do about it. It's not always the same thing – like there is no right answer. You've gotta have your own choice for yourself, don't matter what it is, just be happy with what you've decided … it kind of abbreviates on what I am myself … it's like a shorthand.'

The research interviewer asks: "How long have you been aware of having this internal conversation?"

> 'I've had this for a while. It's from when I was a little child 'cos – I ain't gonna lie, I had trouble when I was a child. No one would talk to me, my parents didn't pay any attention, stuff like that … so I developed a state of mind when the only person I could trust is myself and my head. And my head tells me what to do. And I believed in that all the way through my life … I always based my decisions on that.'

Danny, like Charelle, tells us a lot in the preceding short interview extract.

What do we mean by reflexivity?

Our preliminary question – in this chapter – is: how do young people who are in transition from out-of-home care *use reflexivity* to make sense of their worlds, and to navigate through their worlds?

The question is not – emphatically not – how might a chronically adverse childhood and/or adolescence affect the capacity for reflexivity and planning – a (causal) question that might be addressed within a natural science framework.[11]

Rather, the question is different. It is an interpretative[12] question – allowing us to listen carefully to the detailed perspectives, and voices, and the often very hard work of reflexive[13] thinking and feeling, of individual young people during the transition from out-of-home care. In Chapters 3–6 there is a chance to do this in considerable detail.

But what do we mean by reflexivity?

Let us look at two definitions, one from the developmental psychologist Jerome Bruner, and the second from sociologist Margaret Archer.

Jerome Bruner, in his 1990 book *Acts of Meaning*, writes:

> Human *reflexivity*, [may be regarded as] our capacity to turn around on the past and alter the present in its light, or to alter the past in the light of the present. Neither the past nor the present stays fixed in the face of this reflexivity. The 'immense repository' of our past encounters may be rendered salient in different ways as we review them reflexively, or may be changed by reconceptualization.[14]

Do take a moment to re-read Charelle's and Danny's interview extracts in the previous section in the light of Bruner's definition of reflexivity.

But Margaret Archer, in her 2007 book *Making Our Way through the World: Human Reflexivity and Social Mobility*, provides a different definition:

> The key feature of *reflexive* inner dialogue is silently to pose questions to ourselves and to answer them, to speculate about ourselves, any aspect of our environment and, above all, about the relationship between them.[15]

For Archer, the process of internal conversation:

[I]s itself the practice of reflexivity; it is how we do all those things like self- monitoring, self-evaluation and self-commitment. Being reflexive is a human practice; it is something we do rather than some mysterious faculty that we exercise. Internal dialogue is the practice through which we 'make up our minds' by questioning ourselves, clarifying our beliefs and inclinations, diagnosing our situations, deliberating about our concerns and defining our own projects.[16]

Archer has proposed that internal conversations, as a form of human reflexivity, should be regarded as *central* to our understanding of the interplay between agency and real-life social worlds, including the day-to-day realities of adversity, structural inequality, and discrimination. In her words: 'No reflexivity: no society'.[17] In an extended series of books, she gives a highly differentiated picture of how we actively engage (via internal conversations) with our social worlds. For Archer, internal conversations allow 'agents [to] reflexively deliberate upon the social circumstances that they confront'.[18]

What social circumstances do care-experienced young adults confront? See Box 1.2.

Box 1.2: Transition from out-of-home care, and the potential for extended care services

As Mike Stein has summarised recently: 'Research evidence dating back to the 1980s ... shows that many young people's transitions from care to adulthood are both accelerated and compressed, having to cope with major changes in their lives at a younger age and in a shorter time than those in the general population – a process that can contribute to psychological problems in adjustment.'[19]

Indeed, transition from out-of-home care may be regarded as a major life event.[20] As Philip Mendes and Badal Moslehuddin[21] point out, many care-leavers experience *at least three levels* of severe adversity. First, many 'are still recovering from considerable physical, sexual or emotional abuse or neglect prior to entering care'.[22] Second, many care-leavers will have experienced 'inadequacies in state care, including poor-quality caregivers and constant shifts of placement, carers, schools and workers'.[23] (Sadly, in addition, out-of-home care might have implicated further maltreatment.[24]) Third, care-leavers 'are expected to transition directly from childhood dependence to adult self-sufficiency'.[25]

In addition to these three levels of adversity, multiple forms of profound structural inequality are likely to (continue to) disrupt the lives of many young people in transition from out-of-home care. Research shows that young people in transition from care experience complex barriers to post-school education, employment, and finding safe and secure housing.[26]

In addition, and not surprisingly, young people in transition from care are more likely – than those who have not been in care – to experience mental health issues, drug misuse challenges, and involvement with criminal justice systems.[27] Clearly, all these levels and factors – biographical and current; developmental, family,[28] social, socioeconomic – are cross-cutting and interactive.[29]

The overrepresentation of Indigenous young people in out-of-home care populations remains a major issue in a number of jurisdictions. In addition, for Indigenous young people leaving care, there may be disproportionate challenges in finding accommodation, or in contacts with criminal justice, and many other post-colonial intergenerational issues.[30]

Of course the transition from out-of-home care does not stop at some nominated age. Although some young people will find a way to escape some aspects of compounded adversity, and structural inequality, negative impacts of having been in care are likely to continue beyond the 'compressed and accelerated' transition to adulthood.[31] Recent population-based studies show ongoing inequalities and increased relative risk of mortality by a range of causes.[32] In a meta-analysis of prospective cohort studies (conducted in Canada, Finland, and Sweden), children who had been in care had three times the risk of completed suicide during adulthood compared with those who had not been in care.[33] In a Swedish prospective cohort study there was an 3.5 times higher risk of suicide attempts among adults (age 20–63) who had been exposed to out-of-home care compared with those without such experience.[34]

In the African context – see the Special Issue of the journal *Emerging Adulthood* on leaving care, edited by Adrian van Breda and Kwabena Frimpong-Manso[35] and see a recent literature review on care-leaving in the Global South by Frimpong-Manso[36] – many orphans and vulnerable children are taken into care by relatives and community members ('nonformal kinship care'), although some young people will enter residential care. Reasons for placement in care are likely to include orphanhood or poverty.[37] Recent research on leaving care in Africa has brought to light the central importance of focusing on family and social interdependency, tracing and connecting with living birth family members, and the local cultural contexts of leaving care – all topics that the more independence-oriented literatures from the Global North give relatively less priority to.[38]

In a recent international review of care-leaving policy and legislation, Benjamin Strahl and colleagues state:

> Despite the many difficulties care-leavers face, they have access to relatively few services and even fewer legal entitlements, which in some cases are not even actualized in practice. The overwhelming majority of youth in the transition from care to adulthood in the countries in our sample are left to survive on their own at age 18 or younger, even when legislation makes provisions for them to stay in care longer.[39]

Extended care services might provide one foundation for such service development. Extended care services for young people in transition from care, in which young people are permitted to remain in their care placements beyond age 18, are beginning to be seen in some jurisdictions.[40] In a recent international review of such services by Adrian D. van Breda and colleagues, it was clear that such services, where present, are at an early stage of development, implementation, and evaluation.[41]

Following international political theorist, Afsoun Afsahi's[42] discussion of the notion of *most-deeply affected*, by which she refers to historic injustice, current minoritisation, and states' decisions about legitimacy, young people in care and those in transition from out-of-home care may be regarded as especially vulnerable, a point that underscores the importance of keeping alive the voices of young people in care and leaving care for social justice.[43]

Reflexivity and internal conversations

As Charles Fernyhough says in his influential book *The Voices Within: The History and Science of How We Talk to Ourselves*: 'Talking to yourself in your head is an ordinary activity, and regular folk recognise it when they see it. Not only that, but they also recognise its private qualities ... I never fail to be amazed by this quality of consciousness.'[44]

As discussed earlier, Margaret Archer has proposed that internal conversations, as a form of human reflexivity, should be regarded as *central* to our understanding of the interplay between agency and real-life social worlds. Her work provided the rich theoretical starting point for our studies with young people in transition from out-of-home care (see Box 1.3). Her theoretical framework provides a rare and detailed account of how agency and reflexivity *interplay* with social and cultural context.[45] Her framework foregrounds internal conversations, and in her first study Archer developed an innovative open-ended qualitative interview method[46] to provide participants with an opportunity to reflect on, and discuss, their own internal conversations. We used Archer's interview method in our studies.[47] Charelle and Danny (mentioned earlier) were two participants in our first study.

Reflexivity and what matters during the transition from care

As a key part of her theoretical framework, Margaret Archer suggests that we use our reflexive internal conversations to articulate and define our own unique 'configuration of concerns' – our own accounts of what matters and who matters in our current day-to-day lives.

We found, during our pilot research with the internal conversations interview, that the term 'concerns' – used at several points in the interview protocol[48] and throughout Archer's theoretical work – was confusing, whereas the wording of the original Archer interview question – 'Which areas of your life matter most to you at the moment?'[49] – was crystal clear to participants. Therefore, throughout this book we refer to this crucial and foundational aspect of Archer's work, and our own work, as *what matters*, not as concerns or current concerns.[50]

For Charelle (who we have already met), what matters is:

'At the moment, myself. Myself obviously because I've got to think ... how my rent's being paid, how I'm budgeting. I've got to think of myself at the moment 'cos I'm not working so I've got to think of where my life's going. So, myself, yeah ... I'm going to college September ... I'm looking into doing some volunteer work.'

She then discusses her birth family and the deleterious impact of having lost meaningful emotional contact during childhood – and how much this *matters*:

'Obviously not having my mum around is always going to affect me and being in care is always going to affect me and affect how I think and feel about things, how my relationships are and everything, do you know what I mean? But that, that will always affect me, and it will affect everyone else who's around me as well.'

We discuss in much more detail Charelle's extended sense of what matters in Chapter 4.

Let us take one more example of what matters for another young person from our first study. Brittany, a woman aged 19, is in transition from care: she is currently in her own accommodation but had been in foster care since infancy. She left school at 16, and is currently attending an 8-week course, which is the first education she has received since leaving school. She has no experience of work.

For Brittany[51] what mattered most was: "My [foster] nieces, my [foster] nephews, and getting my house sorted." On reflection, Brittany explains: "I suppose in a way, in my head, because I went through what I went through, I don't want them [foster nieces and nephews] to feel even the slightest similarity to what I went through, so I make sure they don't."

Bruner's definition of reflexivity is again relevant here.

Reflexivity and planning during the transition from care

For Archer, as a pivot of her theoretical model, a clear sense of what matters *makes possible our active engagement with the real social world.* Planned 'courses of action', projects, become possible: "What specifically do we intend to do?"[52] Via internal conversations we adjust and tailor our subjective range of what matters, and our potential courses of action, to what is possible in the real world.

Archer contrasts what she regards as active (that is, planful) agency, with passive agency. She suggests that active agents (that is, actively agential people) show clarity of what matters, and exercise careful 'dovetailing' of their personal configuration or range of aspects of what matters, whereas passive agents (in Archer's account) show uncertainty about their range of what matters, failure of dovetailing, and therefore seem to show an 'absence of strict personal identity, which precludes the prioritisation and accommodation of concerns [what matters] and this blocks the formation of projects'.[53]

For Archer, an agent's (or person's) lack of clarity about what matters translates into a lack of clarity about how to plan (for the future) and act in the world.

In our own research with care-leavers this aspect of Archer's theoretical model seemed not to apply. On the one hand, participants showed great clarity (and *detail*) about what matters, and, on the other hand, were sceptical about forward planning. As we pointed out in our first paper,[54] ' "green shoots" of potential sources of active agency' were evident in the transcripts of each of the participants who, while seeming to have little or no future orientation, had perfectly clear (and reflexive) specification of what (and, importantly, who) mattered most in their lives.

It was as if each of the participants in our studies was re-writing how we might think about agency and reflexivity under conditions of adversity.

There were three aspects of our own findings with young adults experiencing compounded adversity that led us to begin to re-think planning – in particular to re-think it in relation to a young person's reflexive sense of what matters.

First, to repeat, young people in our two studies were deeply sceptical about forward planning. Some rejected future-oriented planning out of hand. We therefore changed the Archer interview protocol (see Box 1.1), during pilot work, to explore participants attitudes to and approaches to planning, giving young people a chance to discuss how they had come to their individual reflexive positions on planning.

Second, to repeat, for participants in our studies there was, on the one hand, clarity of what matters, and, on the other hand, scepticism about forward planning. This did not 'fit' with Archer's model, in which clarity of what matters was integrated (theoretically and practically) with clarity of forward planning. Our data suggest that, at least for some young people with experiences of compounded adversity, we need to unpack what matters and forward-oriented planning. This – unpacking what and who matters, from future orientation and future planning – forms a major aspect of the current book, and we explore this in detail, via young people's own accounts, in Chapters 3–6.

(As discussed in the Introduction, some young people in transition from care will experience an 'integrated' sense of what matters *and* clarity of future-oriented planning – Archerian active agency – perhaps via a sense of ongoing support and/or a sense of relevant skills for the focus of what matters, for example post-school education. Our work does not deny this possibility.[55] Rather, our work aims to understand the perspectives of those young people where this is not the case.)

Third, scepticism about forward planning was sometimes expressed with strong emotion and a strong willingness to account for this position by referring to past experience. We wanted to understand better this expressive clarity (see Chapters 3–7, and see Chapter 10, 'Planning and voice: starting points').

We therefore started to look for formulations of what matters and who matters (as distinct from future-oriented-planning) and we discuss this further throughout this book.

What and who matters became central to the thinking in this book; an alternative to a primary focus on future-oriented goals.

Box 1.3: University of Essex studies of young adults in transition from out-of-home care

In our first study,[56] carried out in a support service for care-leavers in London, England, our research question focused on 'characterising the internal conversations of individual young people in transition from care to an adult independent and interdependent life'.[57] A key issue for our research planning was how to ensure that we, on the one hand, included a wide range of young care-leavers (from those who were in work and/or education and 'achieving', through to those who were 'struggling'), and, on the other hand, kept the numbers of participants to a level that allowed us to do deep micro-analytical analysis of individual interviews, emphasising the central importance of individual patterns of internal conversation and individual voices (see Box 1.4).

The nine participants who consented to participate were diverse on a range of factors – 'achieving' through to struggling, ethnicity, number of family placements, form of housing accommodation, degree of contact with birth family and foster family, sexual orientation, involvement with criminal justice, and mental health issues (we excluded, for ethical reasons, young people who were currently receiving specialist mental health services, but, as we shall see in Chapters 3–7, many of the participants had much to say about aspects of their emotions and mental health, in relation to their internal conversations).

The participants were aged 19–24; of the nine, four were women. The internal conversations interview, which was semi-structured and open-ended, is described in Box 1.1. The data analysis method, which is described in Box 1.4 was interpretative phenomenological analysis (IPA).

The findings of this study on internal conversations, what matters, and planning have briefly been described earlier in this chapter.

In our second study, carried out in collaboration with a leaving care service in Suffolk, UK, our research question focused on how care-leavers make sense of planning and future orientation.[58]

The six participants were aged 18–20; three were women; all were White British, reflecting the low level of ethnic diversity of the study area. The internal conversations interview, which was semi-structured and open-ended, was used, and in addition, young people were invited to discuss their current social networks. The data analysis method, which is described in Box 1.4, was again IPA.

Detailed findings are described in the paper, but for the purposes of this book, five results are of particular significance. First, all participants regarded themselves as preferring not to plan for the future. Second, five out of the six participants discussed detailed and reflexive accounts of how they felt that previous trauma had impacted on their willingness to plan for the future. Third, some participants appeared to conduct short-term, day-to-day/week-to-week life organisation and planning while eschewing planning for the future. Fourth, some of the participants reflected that their internal conversations were unhelpful at times. Fifth, discussions about close relationships – the birth family, romantic relationships, and anxiety and apprehension about loneliness – were a strong feature of the interviews.

In summary, both studies provide new insights into the role of reflexivity in some young people's lives, as young people navigate transition from out-of-home care in two geographic areas of England. As a key part of the reflexive lives of individual young people, what matters, and who matters, may be of distinctive importance in understanding planning agency in the contexts of compounded adversity during emerging adulthood – voices that may not always be heard when we focus solely on future-oriented planning.

Box 1.4: The qualitative analyses: interpretative phenomenological analysis (IPA)[59]

We used IPA in our studies of care-leavers, and I use it in this book (see Chapter 2, and Chapters 3–6). Why? Primarily because there seems to be an 'epistemic fit' between the internal conversations research interview – which Margaret Archer designed to enable participants to discuss their own subjective self-reflections on the detail of their internal and social lives[60] and the underlying principles of IPA, which are concerned with understanding people's individual reflexive meaning-making.[61] In addition to a prime focus on the intricate details of *subjective* experience, IPA is designed to investigate each 'case' – for instance the interview accounts of one person – in great detail. This particular feature of IPA, termed 'idiography',[62] has an especially important 'fit' for our studies in which we have been interested in the distinctive reflexive internal conversations of each individual participant. During analysis we aim to 'hold onto' the 'internal logic', or semantic connections, or narrative voice, or arc of personal meanings, within individual interviews. This approach contrasts with thematically oriented qualitative analysis (including some uses of IPA) which run a risk of losing semantic interconnections in an individual transcript for the sake of overarching across-case study 'themes'.[63]

The micro-analytical/close reading methodological features of IPA mean that sample sizes are usually small or even very small – smaller than in most other types of qualitative study[64] and much smaller than in quantitative studies. Intensive analysis, keeping a focus on the intricacies of meanings in single cases, keeping active comparisons of single cases within a dataset continually in mind, simply isn't possible with a larger dataset. And the purpose of the research – to bring to light the 'subjective work' of individual participants – *is* the purpose of the research.

A reflexive note: those of us doing very small sample qualitative research usually struggle not to write up work in a manner that is 'couched in a discourse of regret or apology' for the small sample sizes![65] It is a useful reminder to recall that our focus in IPA is on understanding people's personal meanings and their meaning-making as a live process. A paper I kept on returning to while engaged in this book was an IPA study of woman's anger and aggression conducted by Virginia Eatough and her colleagues, involving five women participants from an inner-city area of the UK, in which the subjective experience of anger (including bodily experience of anger, escalation, crying and frustration, and other emotions), forms and contexts of aggression (including physical, verbal, indirect, and imagined), and experience of anger as moral judgement (including perceived injustice, and anger as a response to rule violation) 'provide[s] a rich descriptive account of the breadth and complexity of woman's anger and aggression'.[66] The paper attends with care to the accounts of each woman, acknowledges emotion as both visceral and cognitive, and illustrates the principles of IPA in attending to the women's experience as well as their profound self-interpretations of their experience.

A detailed procedural account[67] of how IPA is used in the present book is provided in Chapter 2.

2

Reflexivity reformulated

Preamble

Our qualitative 'descriptive and analytical microscope' – unlike the natural scientist's detailed scrutiny of a leaf or butterfly or blood vessel capillary under a 'physical' or electron microscope – requires us to watch and listen out for the young person's *own voiced account* of their own sense of what and who matters, and their sense of planning and the future. This requirement involves us in what has been called a 'double hermeneutic'[1]– a distinctive aspect of social science, especially qualitative social science – in which the reflexive agency of the participant is taken as the primary focus, *and* we are (also) explicitly aware of our own reflexive lenses as researchers or practitioners.

'No reflexivity: no society'

Margaret Archer's phrase 'No reflexivity; no society'[2] sums up a strong and wonderfully provocative starting point for theorising agency and structure.

Can we, by building on Archer's ideas and work, contribute to the Norwegian social scientist Jan Storø's challenge: 'Given the fact that transitions are personal journeys for these young people [care-leavers], but also embedded in social and structural processes, it would be interesting to see what future researchers can do to bridge between the two linguistic domains.'[3]

In Chapter 1, in addition to describing the multiple struggles care-leavers have to address (see Box 1.2), I asked the question: how do young people who are in transition from out-of-home care use reflexivity *to make sense* of their worlds, and to navigate through their worlds? Margaret Archer's account of reflexivity as internal conversations formed the basis of our thinking, and indeed of the research that we conducted with young adults leaving care.

But there was a sticking point. Archer envisages our individual narratives about what matters as *deeply integral* with planning and organising a life. She argues that clarity about what matters translates into *concrete plans* for 'courses of action'. If I value starting college, then I would logically, within the parameters of her theory, also have a future-oriented plan for how to do that. Clarity and detail of what matters 'equals', in Archer's theoretical perspective, a real-world plan for engaging with the world. The sticking point for our research with young people leaving care was that Archer's 'logical equation' simply did not work, at least for the young people we interviewed. Instead, young people demonstrated a thoughtful and expressive clarity about what and who matters, alongside a scepticism about planning for the future – a scepticism sometimes very strongly expressed.[4]

In Chapter 2 we explore this conundrum in two ways. First I ask: can we picture *reflexivity* more broadly, and more flexibly – might an appreciation of a wider range of forms of reflexivity help us understand better the active uses of reflexivity under conditions of compounded adversity? The first section of this chapter is therefore about a range of different forms of reflexivity – increasing the 'bandwidth' of our appreciation of reflexivity.

Second, I ask, in preparation for the case-based chapters (Chapter 3–6): could a closer, more fine-grained reading of our interview-based qualitative research data on what matters, and on planning, throw more light on how precisely some young people articulate what matters, and consider planning? If the more fine-grained analysis encompassed a broader, more flexible set of ideas about reflexivity (that is, not only internal conversations), would that help us to see more precisely what some young people are articulating/voicing about what matters and about planning?

Let us note that, as is the practice in qualitative research,[5] this researcher had noticed that, although the research interview was about internal conversations, most of the young people's discussions went 'way beyond' internal conversations, as we shall see in Chapters 3–6. Therefore the prompt for broadening the notions of reflexivity and planning comes from the voices of young people themselves – as well as the wider scientific and humanities literature on reflexivity, metacognition, mental time travel, intersubjectivity and shared deliberation, recognition, shared agency, and so on.

So, first, to a broader view of reflexivity, or reflexivities.

Reflexivity on a broader front

Self-reflection

In the internal conversations interview, participants are invited to *reflect on* their own internal conversations, to reflect on what matters – what is most important in their lives at the moment – and to reflect on planning (see Box 1.1). The interview does not, in any sense, provide a 'read-out' of 'data' on a person's internal conversations, or a 'list' of what matters, or an 'itemised' account of a participant's planning. (Nor was it intended to by Margaret Archer.[6]) To repeat, the research participant is invited to be self-reflective about their own internal conversations, about what matters, and about their own stance, or position, on planning. So, what do we usually mean by self-reflection?

In philosopher Simon Blackburn's words:

> Human beings are relentlessly capable of reflecting on themselves. We might do something out of habit, but then we begin to reflect on the habit. We can habitually think things, and then reflect on what we are thinking. We can ask ourselves (or sometimes we get asked by other people) whether we know what we are talking about. To answer that we need to reflect on our own positions, our own understanding of what we are saying.[7]

Or cognitive psychologist Albert Bandura:

> The fourth agentic property [see later for the other three] is self-reflectiveness. People are not only agents of action. They are also self-examiners of their own

functioning. Through functional self-awareness, they reflect on their personal efficacy, the soundness of their thoughts and actions, and the meaning of their pursuits, and they make corrective adjustments if necessary. The metacognitive capability to reflect upon oneself and the adequacy of one's thoughts and actions is the most distinctly human core property of agency.[8]

(On Bandura's account, the four core properties of human agency are intentionality [including planning], forethought [including goal-setting], self-reactiveness [including self-regulation and self-modification of plans], and self-reflectiveness. He also emphasises the 'social embeddedness' of human agency.[9])

Self-reflection is something we all do, as part of day-to-day life. If Bandura is right, it may be regarded as *the* most distinctively human property of agency.

The internal conversations interview requires participants to use this capability in deliberating about and discussing their own experience of internal conversations, what matters, and planning.

Self-reflection about internal conversations led some participants (in both our studies) to discuss their 'struggles' with their own internal conversations (see especially Chapter 3 of this book, and see the findings from our second study[10]).

But, before we become too 'internal', self-reflection is also about our selves as physical bodies: our looks, our appearances, our speaking voices.

Embodiment

Two 'takes' on embodiment, one from philosopher and psychologist Maurice Merleau-Ponty: 'If my arm is resting on the table I should never think of saying that it is beside the ash-tray in the way in which the ash-tray is beside the telephone.'[11]

And a second 'take' from critical geographers, Sofia Zaragocin and Martina Angela Caretta: 'We understand embodiment as lived experiences related to identity, power, location, and materiality as personally and individually known by the research participants and manifested in bodily sensations and emotions.'[12]

Our bodies, obviously, are part of our selves. Yet much philosophical writing has set the body aside, giving priority to the mind, as if it were a separate and perhaps 'precious' space; what Charles Taylor calls a 'notoriously disengaged picture of thinking', and, quoting Elizabeth Anscombe, 'an incorrigibly contemplative conception of knowledge'.[13] 'Internal conversations' might be regarded as one example of this apparently disembodied approach to thinking and feeling.

In his 1945 book *Phenomenology of Perception*, Maurice Merleau-Ponty's chapter titles begin to tell a more embodied story:

> The spatiality of one's own body and motility
> The synthesis of one's own body
> The body in its sexual being
> The body as expression, and speech

So in Chapter 5, Nailah reflects on the effects of racist bullying at school on her current sense of her own facial and physical looks, and how those effects link to other aspects of her current day-to-day life. In Chapter 4, Charelle uses physical, embodied metaphor to reflect on the emotional impact of her disrupted family life: "Like with your parents, your parents, like that's your backbone, they hold you up when you're falling and whatever."

Throughout the interviews participants use voice (and eyes, and face) to express and articulate their feelings about what matters and about planning.

In Bessel van der Kolk's widely cited book on trauma, *The Body Keeps the Score: Mind, Brain and Body in the Transformation of Trauma*, he describes 'losing your body': 'I was amazed to discover how many of my patients [with a diagnosis of post-traumatic stress disorder – PTSD] told me they could not feel whole areas of their bodies.'[14]

Shared deliberation and intersubjectivity

Frédéric Vandenberghe, in a review of Margaret Archer's (2003) *Structure, Agency and the Internal Conversation*, argues that Archer's account of internal conversations:

> [N]eglects intersubjective communication, social movements and democracy. Even if the internal

> conversation is conceptualized as a causal power that transforms both agents and society, only half of the story is told in this book. Foregrounding the morphogenesis of individual agency, the morphogenesis of structure through collective action is hardly touched. The book is about the ethics of existence, but fails to address the politics of life.[15]

In this densely critical few sentences, Vandenberghe picks up several points which we return to throughout this book.[16] However, if we focus simply on his point about 'intersubjective communication', reflexivity, as Vandenberghe clearly indicates, may be *shared* – at least some of the time: social, cooperative, disputative, deliberative, potentially democratic.

For research participants in our studies, were specific decisions *shared*? Were friends or family consulted about particular concerns or dilemmas? The answer is yes – with family – see Chapter 3, and friends – see Chapters 4, 5, and 6. For Zavie, who discussed the importance of the 'safety network' of friends, "it's a circle of building up trust and it being broken down and building up trust and being broken down again". This, he found, was something he/we "constantly talked about with our friends" (Chapter 6).

We discuss this collaborative aspect of reflexivity in Chapter 8, as part of a detailed account of Michael Bratman's theoretical work in which he argues for 'a deep *continuity* between individual and social agency'.[17] Bratman refers to our capacity for being 'doubly reflexive';[18] reflexive both in a first-person sense, and as a 'we'. Zavie, discussed earlier, talks about his own reflexive view, but at the same time says: "I wouldn't say it is anything to do with me" and goes on to discuss his experience of 'we' and 'us' in the specific context of a long-standing friendship group.

Let us note, revisiting Box 1.2 on compounded adversity and the transition from care, that this is an aspect of life (being socially together, sometimes in shared deliberation, sometimes in sheer enjoyment, and of course in attachment relationships) in which the participant may have been maltreated, unprotected, and repeatedly unsupported,[19] but equally an area which may be of especial personal importance – part of what matters and of course who matters.

Let us note also that the interview, although nominally about internal conversations, did give, in its open-ended design, an opportunity for young people to talk about *shared* deliberations, which, as we shall see in Chapters 3–7, they frequently did.

We have mentioned several times the young person's *autobiographical* sense of what matters and who matters, and Bruner's definition of reflexivity[20] (see Chapter 1) includes a sense of the interplay between the remembered past and the present. But can we be more precise about the process of reflecting on time and autobiography?

Mental time travel

Our reflexivities are embedded and embodied in time. As Jerome Bruner describes so eloquently,[21] we picture our own past time, the rough and ever-changing present time, and sometimes we deliberate on our future time. Our plans, or attempts at plans, are inserted into the sometimes chaotic world around us.

Young people repeatedly discussed autobiographical past time during the internal conversations interviews,[22] and sometimes declined to discuss future time (see Chapter 1).

Focusing on autobiographical/subjective time, let us allow ourselves to be drawn into the deeply fascinating concept of mental time travel. Can we use the concept of mental time travel to begin to understand some young people's articulate self-interpretations of past experience, *and* parallel rejection of the notion of future-oriented planning?

The cognitive neuroscience-based idea of mental time travel is that memory systems evolved (in an evolutionary or natural selection sense) so that we, and indeed some other animals, can plan for the future.[23] Memory is regarded not as something entirely focused on the remembered past, but memory as something that allows us to build on experience *in order to sensibly plan for the future*. In the words of the cognitive neuroscientist Arnaud D'Argembeau: 'While memory obviously refers to the past, from an evolutionary perspective, its fundamental function is to aid the organism in anticipating and planning for the future. Surprisingly, however, it is only quite recently that empirical research on future-oriented thinking has taken off.'[24]

D'Argembeau has defined mental time travel as the 'capacity to flexibly navigate layers of autobiographical representations at multiple timescales, from broad lifetime periods that span years to short-time slices of experience that span seconds'.[25]

Reflexive representations of the personal past are integrated with potential future scenarios, fuelling imagination, and guiding decision-making and planning. Central is the notion of a 'personal timeline scaffolded from conceptual knowledge of the content and structure of our life'.[26]

In Chapter 8 we discuss the implications of this idea (and a wide range of other time-related ideas) for understanding the active and reflexive interpretations and personal timelines of young people experiencing compounded adversity.

Moving forward to the next section of this chapter, I prepare the ground for the case-based chapters, which I see as standing at the heart of this book.

A closer reading of participants' discussions of what matters and of planning

In this section I prepare the ground for Chapters 3–6, in which I report a secondary analysis of the interviews conducted in our first study of young people in transition from care in London (see Box 1.3[27]). Building on the wider range of forms/aspects of reflexivity discussed in this chapter, the research question I address in Chapters 3–6 is: how do individual young people use their capacities for multifaceted reflexivity – including self-reflection, embodiment, shared deliberation, mental time travel – to articulate what matters, and to formulate a stance/position on planning, including future/forward planning?

I will prepare the ground in two ways. First, I will briefly introduce and suggest a flexible – and I hope creative – way of reading Chapters 3–6. Second, I will dig deeper, and outline the method and methodology of the qualitative approach used in these case-based chapters.

Reading Chapters 3–6: a rough and flexible guide

1. To get the most out of Chapters 3–6, I suggest (re)-reading Boxes 1.1–1.4 in Chapter 1. These boxes outline the internal conversations interview framework (Box 1.1), what transition

from care entails (Box 1.2), the findings from our two primary studies (Box 1.3), and the qualitative inquiry method: interpretative phenomenological analysis (IPA; Box 1.4).

2. In qualitative data analysis, such as IPA,[28] researchers *immerse* themselves by reading and re-reading the data transcripts and/or listening repeatedly to the audio-recordings of the interviews. You become absorbed and occupied with the young people's narratives, trying hard not to leap to conclusions, or to apply strong theoretical models, or to apply diagnostic frameworks, or to tick mental boxes. As readers of Chapters 3–6, you may want to echo that process by first reading and re-reading just Chapter 3, allowing the findings gradually to interplay with your own experience, before moving on to Chapter 4. Spoiler alert – Chapter 4 provides a strong contrast with Chapter 3, so there is much to be gained by deeply engaging with Chapter 3 first.

3. It will be helpful to try to keep the research question in mind as you are reading Chapter 3: that is, how do individual young people use their capacities for multifaceted reflexivity – including self-reflection, embodiment, shared deliberation, mental time travel – to articulate what matters, and to formulate a stance/position/personal logic on planning – including future/forward planning? We are trying to understand much more about 'the way' young people are so precise and expressive and emotional and vocal about what and who matters, and to understand much more about their individual 'approaches' to planning. Each chapter gives space for *individual voices*, and comparison between two individual voices, each with apparently similar foci of what or who matters. In Chapter 3 it is 'family matters'.

4. Immersing oneself in transcripts, or indeed immersing ourselves as readers in each of these case-based chapters, can be like reading parts of an autobiography or biography. So we try, empathically and non-judgementally (I'm sure readers of this book couldn't be judgemental), to 'tune into' the young person and her or his narrative.

5. Once you feel from reading just Chapter 3 that you have appreciated the complex and multiple-reflexive accounts of what matters and approaches to planning for Corrina and Brittany

(pseudonyms), you may (!) move on to Chapter 4, to meet Charelle and Danny. And so on to Chapters 5 and 6, each of which provides fascinating contrasts on what matters and on a range of forms of reflexive and individual approaches to planning.

6. One of the many joys of qualitative analysis – especially IPA – can be that you begin to appreciate each individual young person on their own terms. This is a useful bar to set for oneself as a reader: have I managed to read these narratives in the terms of the young persons themselves?

Reading Chapters 3–6 – a slightly more technical guide

Here I will discuss the analytical qualitative research method I have used in the secondary analysis in Chapters 3–6 in some detail, paying careful attention to the need for transparency in the method. Why transparency? As psychologist Rivka Tuval-Mashiach (2017) suggests:

> Methodological flexibility in qualitative research is not only unavoidable but also an inherent part of it. Each case of qualitative research is a singular process, requiring the researcher to craft his or her own method or make changes in accordance with the circumstances. As a result, the study's process and decisions taken along the way often remain obscure to the reader.[29]

Indeed there are a number of novel aspects to our published studies and to the secondary analysis reported in Chapters 3–6: first, the internal conversations interview itself, which not only focuses on 'lived experience' but also young people's *self-reflections on their lived experience*; second, the analysis methodology – interpretative phenomenological analysis (IPA) – utilised here in these case-based chapters in a specific way that maximises the researcher's attention to idiographic aspects of the data; third, our attention to expressive/emotional aspects of young people's narratives, rather than only naming or designative or thematic aspects of language; and fourth, the epistemological context – aspect realism – which is particularly novel, and affects all levels of the analysis in Chapters 3–6.

The specific study this secondary analysis is based on is Study 1 (Hung and Appleton, 2016; and see Boxes 1.1–1.4),[30] which included nine young adults (aged between 19 and 24) who were in the process of transitioning from out-of-home care in an area of London, England, and who were diverse in terms of gender, ethnicity, sexual orientation, number of placements, accommodation, education, and involvement with criminal justice systems. The young adults were interviewed using the internal conversations interview framework. In the first interview the young person was invited to discuss their own patterns of internal conversations. In the second interview (conducted several days or weeks after the first) there was a focus on what matters, and on planning.

In this secondary analysis, I focus on eight of the nine participants as one participant's account of what matters and who matters was so strongly identifiable that confidentiality would potentially have been breached.

In the secondary analysis reported in this book, interpretative phenomenological analysis (IPA) was used, emphasising participants' active, expressive, and reflexive meaning-making.[31] I build on Jonathan Smith's[32] recent and innovative formulation of IPA in five linked ways: idiography, the exact context of the interview, a participant's personal logic, expressive and emotion-based aspects of interviews, and aspect realism and 'respecting the hustle'.

Idiography

In the IPA analysis (in Chapters 3–6) I focus on idiographic aspects of analysis (the particular individual, her particular experience, the particular interview focusing on internal conversations, what matters, and planning; see Chapter 1, Box 1.3), with initial close reading and re-reading of individual transcripts, and, as a second stage, I use qualitative paired case comparison[33] to compare and contrast pairs of cases in which the focus of what matters appeared similar, but in which there were interesting and informative contrasts in each of the aspects of interest. The point of paired case comparison is to draw out 'spaces of contrast',[34] sustaining our ear for *individual reflexive voices*, and drawing attention to disparity between individuals with an apparently similar sense of what and who matters. Because of the idiographic focus of the analysis, there is no attempt to move to the later stages of IPA,[35] which usually involves across-case thematic analysis.[36]

The exact context of the interview(s)

I use a heightened awareness of the precise internal conversations interview (see Chapter 1, Box 1.1) context – for instance asking at what point in the two interviews did the participant discuss such and such? To take an example, 'what and who matters' was frequently discussed at points in the interviews other than when the interview question was asked about 'what matters'. What sense do we make of specific instances of this?

The internal conversations interview does not *specifically* ask participants to describe social and intersubjective aspects of reflexivity (for instance, the interview *could* – but doesn't – ask: Who do you *share* your internal conversations with? Who do you 'plan together' with?). But the interview is semi-structured and open-ended, and it is informative that participants very frequently described a range of social/intersubjective aspects of reflexivity, shared deliberation, and who matters.[37]

A participant's personal logic

I draw out examples of highly individual 'internal' or 'inner', or personal logic, or 'phenomenological logic',[38] or characterisation,[39] or autobiographical logic, to a participant's narrative about an event or experience, or about what and who matters, or about the future and/or planning. In Chapter 3, both participants explain their own 'logics' for what and who matters. For an extended example of a complex and meaningful 'logic', read Nailah's account in Chapter 5 of her personal sense of time during the period running up to transition from out-of-home care, and during transition (incorporating not only self-reflection and mental time travel, but also embodied metaphors, and a very strong sense of the importance of intersubjectivity and shared deliberation[40]).

Expressive and emotion-based aspects of interviews

Articulation by individual participants is a *live*, sometimes dramatic,[41] vivid, self-discovering, sometimes ironic, and sometimes highly expressive experience – emotion in real time, at particular points in the interview. Some highly emotional experiences will be immensely difficult for participants to articulate or 'pin down' – the experience may seem 'inchoate'[42] to the participant, or may appear contradictory ('illogical') to the interviewer. The interviewer may have tried to facilitate the participant in clarifying their own evolving sense of meaning of the experience. Expressive aspects of language are actively used in the analysis. What might we mean by 'expressive'? The question is important because both researchers and practitioners are familiar with expressive and sometimes upsetting 'material' in interviews, but research methods often 'reduce' this to names of emotions (anxiety, anger), names of problems (domestic violence), names of mental health disorders (post-traumatic stress disorder – PTSD), and names of strategies (de-escalation). How can we 'tune in' – both in research and in practice – to the *language* of expressive and emotion-based discussion? In a ground-breaking book, *The Language Animal: The Full Shape of Human Linguistic Capacity* (2016), the Canadian philosopher Charles Taylor makes a distinction between two approaches to (or aspects of?) language – the designative-instrumental, and the expressive-constitutive. The first is in a sense very familiar – the words we use refer to objects, events, people, themes – and these words usually have a shared cultural background of meaning. Our day-to-day lives depend on our ability to use this crucial aspect of language. The second approach, also very familiar, is evident in theatre, soap-operas, music theatre, dance, stand-up, poetry, and in our day-to-day expressive lives that go beyond 'just words'. If a young person says she is angry about having been let down by the system, the word 'angry' here is, of course, expressive. A word, in the designative account of language, may or may not 'matter' to the person using it, but in the expressive account, a word not only matters, but is linked to feeling, and often linked to a 'logical' web of interconnected personal thoughts, feelings, and ideas about what matters in one's own life, and in the lives of those close to one. In

Charles Taylor's words, referring to meanings that have expressive, personal or value-based contexts: 'There is no *dispassionate* access to these meanings ... understanding them is grasping their point, the point they have for those who live by them.'[43] Finally, time past, time present, and time future may be seen designatively – attending to the precision of dating, and clarity of time-based description in words – recall, for instance, of the date and place of being taken into care, or considering a future-oriented event such as starting a new college course at a particular date later in the year. And time may also be seen *expressively*. A key question in this book is: how might an expressive approach to language help us think about reluctance to plan for the future?

Aspect realism and 'respecting the hustle'

The philosophical (or 'epistemological') positioning of this approach is perhaps best termed as aspect realism. The Wittgensteinian philosopher Juliet Floyd describes aspect realism as: 'without grounded metaphysics and no particular epistemology or theory of mind'.[44]

For Floyd, 'aspects are modal, attaching to possibilities and necessities: fields of significance, opportunities for projecting and instantiating our concepts'.

She advocates very careful attention to the 'rough ground' of ordinary day-to-day language: aspect perception not as a psychological phenomenon, but as part of forms of life, as a way of structuring possible lives, based on real-life experience and real social worlds. In the context of our focus in this book on interpretations of severe and compounded adversity (see Box 1.2), during emerging adulthood we may picture the young person as having experienced 'possibilities and necessities', and constructed 'fields of significance' based on engagement with their own real-lifeworlds. Aspects are indeed from real life, *and* they are self-reflexively interpreted – by the young person herself, sometimes together with others. There is an opportunity to voice and project those ideas during the research interview, and, we might hope, during day-to-day real life.

Self-reflection is key for Floyd: 'We see *through* the picture to our own seeing of it *as* realizing one way among others.

What we see is seen, but also we see. We rearticulate what we see, sometimes seeing it thereby anew. There is an active and a passive aspect to this.'[45] There is formulation, reformulation, reinterpretation, and ongoing puzzlement. For Floyd: 'We should respect the hustle'[46]

Aspect realism regards the phenomena young people talk about as real. The 'instability' of frequent placement moves happened. The maltreatment happened. The violence and drug-misuse in the neighbourhood is happening, and it is affecting my day-to-day life. Interpretations by the young person are works in progress – they involve 'assembling and re-assembling'. There will be contradictions. Planning what to do in the future of my life might have to come later – or not at all – because of real-life contingencies *and* perceptions of contingencies.

Aspect realism has many overlaps with social constructionism – in particular an aversion to 'essentialism', respect for human meanings and understandings as being central to human activity, the embeddedness of meaning-making in specific times and places (and 'cultures'), and a critical perspective.[47] Aspect realism, on the other hand, might not necessarily argue that 'meaning and understanding have their beginnings in social interaction, in shared agreements as to what these symbolic forms are to be taken to be'.[48] And the question: 'Is there a real world outside discourse?' gets a whole chapter in Vivien Burr's immensely helpful book on social constructionism.[49]

For critical realism (CR) 'there is nothing that is not real'.[50] In a 'maximally inclusive ontology'[51] conceptualisations (and internal conversations) are one part of a layered or 'stratified' ontology involving multiple levels and modes of engagement between knower and known.[52] For Margaret Archer, as one proponent (and contributory founder) of critical realism, it is possible to understand structure and agency as ontologically and analytically distinct, and unfolding over time. Her work examines the *interplay* between ontologically distinct levels, and over time.[53] CR seems to differ from aspect realism in one major foundational aspect, that is, that CR has very specific metaphysical positions, and is frequently critical of social constructionism.[54] In stark contrast, aspect realism deliberately makes no metaphysical assumptions. But – let us also note the wide range of ideas in CR – Vandenberghe has recently argued for what he calls a 'critical realist hermeneutics', in which he notes the importance for 'old school' CR to 'welcome and digest contributions from deconstruction, social constructivism, neo-Kantianism, feminism and post-colonialism'.[55]

Lakshman Wimalasena's CR research in postcolonial Sri Lanka provides a helpful example of how Archer's account of the role of reflexivity in social context can throw light on the 'diversity associated with conscious human action that can recognise the voice of the subaltern' and 'allows deeper insights into the concealed realities beyond the assumption that subaltern is a passive actor, a product of society'.[56]

One aspect of aspect realism is of special relevance to our analysis in Chapters 3–6: Juliet Floyd's account of Wittgenstein's notion of logic as an integral part of our forms of life, or 'possibilities of life-structuring in life',[57] and 'the *speaking* of language is part of an activity, or of a form of life'.[58] If we think of participants' narratives as chains of reasoning with which a young person attempts to scaffold her understanding of her real world, and fashion links in her real world, then this logic, and the articulation of this logic, is a key starting point of the research – drawing out 'aspects of thoughts, given in fields of necessity, contingency, and possibility that we can take in'.[59] (See Chapter 8 for further discussion of the relevance of Floyd's account of logic for this research, and its relevance to practice.) Our acknowledgement of each chain of reasoning, each expression of personal logic, each voice, is an acknowledgement of knowledge of particular circumstances, with the chain of reasoning seen as part of that form of life. Aspects (of the real world, and the imagined world), as seen by participants in their own lives, are *given life* by the young person as she attempts to embed those ideas in her day-to-day life, and sometimes in her sense of her future, and as she voices those chains of linked ideas to others. The talk is essential to the work of being – it is not decorative, or secondary to the 'real world'. These aspects are newfangled forms of life; this is part of the real world. For aspect realism, *how* we voice, articulate, and link (whether participant or researcher or practitioner), what we specifically do *in* linking, is constitutive, is part of reality, then to be returned to, rearranged, and discussed with those we care about, or care for us.

Structure of each chapter in Chapters 3–6

In addressing the question about how individual young people use their capacities for multifaceted reflexivity to articulate what matters, and to formulate a stance/position/personal logic on planning, each chapter (in Chapters 3–6) focuses on just two individuals – the paired case comparison method mentioned earlier.

Individual 'voices' are discussed in a first section of each chapter, and paired comparison in the second section.

Each of the four chapters focuses on a personally important aspect of what or who matters which appeared similar or comparable for two individuals:

- Chapter 3: My family matters
- Chapter 4: A roof over my head: self-reliance matters
- Chapter 5: Time future: time complex
- Chapter 6: What matters is social: friendships and social responsibility

3

My family matters

How do individual young people use their capacities for multifaceted reflexivity – including self-reflection, embodiment, shared deliberation, and mental time travel – to articulate what matters, and to formulate a stance/position on planning – including future/forward planning?

Corrina

Corrina, aged 20, is a woman in transition from care, who has been in foster care for seven years after severe maltreatment and neglect. While in transition, she has gained some previous experience of an apprenticeship, but is currently looking for work. (We have discussed Corrina very briefly in the Introduction.)

Corrina was asked the question 'Which areas of your life matter most to you at the moment?'[1]

Corrina:	Um … my family, er … my friends.
Interviewer:	Anything else?
Corrina:	I want to go to college. I want to go in September.

Expanding, Corrina explained that she wanted to study childcare and eventually become a social worker. Her previous foster carer had come to a further education open day with her and helped her make the decision about what course to apply for.

The interviewer asked about family and its importance to her. By family she meant both her foster family and her birth family.[2] She had been estranged from her birth mother and father for some years. Recently her birth father had been in touch and wanted to meet up. She described the complex decision. It involved talking with trusted friends and family, and internal dialogue. In particular she was helped in her decision by imagining what her recently deceased paternal grandfather might have advised.

Later in the second interview – after the discussion of 'what matters' – the researcher asked:

Interviewer:	[Is there] anything that's made family so important to you?
Corrina:	Well, like – before it was always my Grandad; he was always my – he was – he was the one that always knew everything and always spoke to me and stuff and when he passed away [12 months ago] I felt like I didn't have anyone to talk to but like when I spoke to Dad, I kind of felt a lot better … my Grandad always wanted me and my Dad to talk one day so now we've done it.

In the first interview Corrina had said: "I always think of my Grandad. I always think 'what would he say?' Yeah. He was the closest person. Like, more than my Dad."

Family, for Corrina, included her foster carer: "She, like you know, helped me and stuff – like she was my Mum like, I didn't see my Mum so like she did everything a Mum would do."

Corrina discussed several members of her birth and foster family members during the two interviews, underscoring the importance they had in her sense of her current life. During the first interview she said: "They [family] come first".

However, her feelings were understandably conflicted. At one point, in the middle of the second interview, she says: "No, I don't get on with my family at all." Unpacking this she explained that some birth family members had recently relocated, which had reminded her of when she had been placed in care and had been separated from her birth siblings. She remembers feeling that she was "like the outcast, sort of thing … I've always felt like that but now I can see that I'm not."

In both interviews Corrina explained that she did not plan: "No, not really 'cos it never goes to plan anyway. I can't plan, I have to do it the day before. I can't 'cos I don't know if I'm going to feel [describes anxiety issues] so I have to plan on the day."

Her sense of *not* planning includes both longer-term planning ("I can't imagine the future") and more immediate practical planning for the following day. For instance, when asked about *rehearsing* (one of the prompt questions in the internal conversations interview) she says: "I don't. I never do. I don't. I just say it."

Corrina mentions her mental health issues early in the first interview. She regards her internal conversations as helping her manage these, both by herself, and also by regularly discussing her recurrent and sometimes disabling worries and occasional suicidal ideation with certain other members of her family, and her key worker – "I think about it first, and then tell someone after". In a sense of shared deliberation, specific family members are key to her sense of managing her day-to-day mental health issues.

What matters is not only family, but also friends. Internal conversations do seem to be less important than being with and speaking with friends and confidantes. As she says in the first interview when asked about whether she uses internal conversations to do day-to-day problem-solving: "I talk to others."

Brittany

Brittany, aged 19, is a woman in transition from care. She had been in foster care since infancy, and had left school at the age of 16, but currently she is living in her own accommodation and is attending an 8-week course, her first post-school education. She has no experience of work.

For Brittany what mattered most was: "My [foster] nieces, my [foster] nephews, and getting my house sorted." On reflection, Brittany explains: "I suppose in a way, in my head, because I went through what I went through, I don't want them [foster nieces and nephews] to feel even the slightest similarity to what I went through, so I make sure they don't." She had enjoyed helping with her foster brother's children for some time: "I liked playing with them and helping change their nappies and stuff."

Thinking about what matters about her new accommodation, she recalls her most recent (and her first) independent accommodation – a shared house where, she gradually realised there was drug-dealing: "Well, yeah, because for three months while it was happening, I didn't do anything. I just let them take the piss, and I let them bring drugs to my house. In my head I was thinking, 'Brittany you're an idiot'."

A woman-friend of her ex-foster mother helped her make a final decision about finding some new accommodation. Now, in her new accommodation, she is "saving up and buying things I need", ensuring she pays for fuel, and "make it a home, make it look pretty". Although she doesn't have a bank account – and explains that she doesn't have a copy of a birth certificate or passport – she is *actively* thinking about money: "Like my [foster family member] works mad hours ... he does some stupid [long] shifts and is on call-out ... I don't think he gets what he deserves ... [specifies wage packet amount] ... but its nicer to know you've earned your money."

On future-oriented planning, she is quite clear: "I can't. I told you that. I plan for today. 'Cos in my head, 'cos I lost [a family member who died 3 years previously] and since then I don't plan for tomorrow. I don't plan for the future. I live for today."

She reflects about her loss: "Me and him were the closest." And: "I don't really think long-term. My [ex-foster mother] gets annoyed with me about this."

Interviewer: How do you feel about the future?

Brittany: Don't know. I don't really think about it apart from when I come to this centre 'cos I'm made to [refers to pathway/transition planning]. Other than that, my head's blank. I don't think about it and take each day as it comes.

Interviewer: What about your [foster] nieces and [foster] nephews, do you imagine things for them?

Brittany: Yeah, I want them to have a good life and stick to things I didn't. To have ten GCSEs (UK national high/secondary school exams) rather than three, and things like that.

She feels more secure than she used to, and reflects, during the interview, on how her 'approach' to life had changed. She recalls 'running away' from her foster home and having been a 'rude child'. But now: "It don't get you nowhere being rude – no-one will respect you for it … I just grew up." She also actively remembers, during the second interview, how her foster mother had tried to prepare her for transition:

> 'Well, I was warned and warned and warned for years by my [foster] mum. She warned me: "Brittany, when you do move, you're going to find this hard, 'cos you don't listen to nothing I say to you and you think I'm mad when I moan at you about the things you need to do", which I did. I used to tell her to shut up when she moaned at me but moving out opened my eyes 'cos now I've got to do it for myself. I can't hide behind my mum and let her pay the rent.'

She is now independent, but also deeply connected to her wider [foster] family, partly via her provision of regular childcare, which she sees as of central importance to her.

Despite the deeply thoughtful sections of the interviews about family and about "getting my house sorted", Brittany regarded much of her internal conversation as focused on "just annoying things". She also self-reflects that her internal conversations had been of no use in dealing with the drug-dealing in her previous accommodation: "It didn't help me at all, my internal conversation."

Comparison

Articulating what/who matters

Both young people were able to articulate, without doubt, matters that were personally important to them. Both identified particular aspects of family. In addition, Corrina identified a possible college course. Brittany identified holding onto and making good her new accommodation.

A major part of Brittany's narrative about the new accommodation was the contrast she saw with her previous shared home, where on-site drug-dealing by her peers had been a major problem (she felt, on reflection, that she had not known how to think about or manage this). Her clarity about the present – how important the new accommodation is – was reflexively informed by (mental time travel) accounts of what had happened 'last time' with accommodation.

Each talked in considerable detail about specific family (and foster family) members, relationships with them, and how those relationships made sense *in terms of past experience*. Examples include: the strong commitment Brittany has to her foster nieces and nephews, and *why*; the imaginative role Corrina gives to the mental picture she has of her deceased grandfather in working out how to relate to her birth father; the detailed account Brittany gives of her current reflections on her foster mother's attempts to socialise her, and her remembered responses!

Importantly, articulation of what matters did not always mean 'internal consistency'. Corrina, during the second interview, says, "No, I don't get on with my family at all". Given the chance to talk around this, she recalls having felt like "an outcast", but "now I can see that I'm not". She uses the opportunity of the interview to explain reflexively and precisely what she means. What initially seems contradictory (to the interviewer) makes sense when the young person explains the autobiographical/mental time travel context, for her.

(I note that 'contradiction' or 'conflicted' did not enter this analysis as a separate major aspect/category/theme, but rather as *an integral part of articulating what and who matters*. I return to this in Chapter 4 with Danny's self-reliant – and sometimes apparently self-contradictory – account of what matters.)

And indeed, for Brittany and Corrina, what and who mattered included the close involvement of significant others in *being together* and/or 'thinking together' – the intersubjective/shared deliberation aspects of reflexivity.[3]

I want to pick up *four aspects of shared deliberation* in relation to these two participants:

First, family matters, not only as a 'focus' of internal reflection about what matters, but also as a 'place' where deliberations – thoughts and feelings and wishes – are shared – where there is 'common ground' and shared history, and a reflexive sense of 'we'.

Corrina is especially pleased to be back in regular touch with her birth siblings, from whom she was separated while being in care. For Brittany, *being with* her [foster] nieces and nephews is central to her life. After losing a foster family member a few years previously she remembers "a good [foster] family unit around me", and "it's easier to talk to someone who's been through it, who's suffered the same loss". Feeling part of a family was central to both young women. Corrina recalled having previously felt "the outcast sort of thing ... but now I can see that I am not".

Second, Corrina preferred talking with others, rather than internally conversing with herself. She identified people in her family and social network with whom she talked about specific matters – she knew who to go to in order to talk about particular sorts of concerns. Shared discussions, for Corrina, seemed more important than her own internal conversations, which at least some of the time, were distressing and disabling[4] – she used her self-awareness of the onset of anxiety symptoms to signal that she should talk to trusted others.

Third, a woman-friend of her ex-foster mother helped Brittany make a final decision about finding some new accommodation.

Fourth, Corrina *imagined* what her deceased grandfather might say about something that concerned her. In one sense of course this is not social, not 'we', but in another sense, it is – he *figured* in her life and he 'mentally exists' as someone whom she can trust. The imaginative/ intersubjective/mental time travel memory of him helped her decide whether to re-admit her birth father into her family network.

The clarity with which the two young people in this chapter spoke of the importance of *shared* deliberation (as distinct from internal conversations) fits with Michael Bratman's 'remarkable trio' account of planning, which I discuss in Chapter 8. And, as we shall see, even the two avowedly self-reliant participants discussed in Chapter 4 had much to say about what matters/who matters in social and family life, and the conditions under which shared deliberation was important.[5]

Planning

Brittany organised her day-to-day and week-to-week life around travelling, on an agreed schedule, to care for her foster nieces and nephews. She also intended to "keep on top of" looking after her new accommodation – payments, upkeep, and so on (a form of short-term planning/everyday planning?).

Corrina not only valued her family and friends but had negotiated with them in practical terms whether and how to re-admit her birth father into her family network. She certainly had to dig deep into her own thoughts and feelings about what mattered most in her life, recall memories of her father and how he had treated her, and imagine her paternal grandfather's 'voice'. But crucially, in what we are terming *shared deliberation*, she had also *talked with* her grandmother and trusted friends about the decision.

Interestingly, toward the end of the second interview, after she has explained that she does not plan, the research interviewer asks about keeping in touch with her father:

Interviewer:	So would you be saying [to yourself] "I haven't seen my dad for a week, I want to see him?"
Corrina:	Yeah, 'cos we're always, we always try to plan it so we know what day we're meeting and stuff.

Although this seems to be in contradiction with what Corrina says about future planning, it does help us understand how she does indeed organise and structure day-to-day life based on what matters (and even including the use of the word 'plan').

Both Brittany and Corrina insisted that they did not forward plan. This expressive clarity – forceful and exclaiming – about *not* wishing to forward plan is an aspect of 'language about planning' that I return to in Chapter 4, and then in Chapters 8–10.

A set of *reflexive* reasons – a personal logic – is given for not wishing to forward plan. For Corrina this included both her previous experience of "things not working out", and current day-to-day specific mental health issues. For Brittany she mentions the recent loss of a loved family member.

4

A roof over my head: self-reliance matters

In Chapter 3 Brittany and Corrina reflexively explained how their families (birth family and foster family) were of primary importance to them.

In this chapter I discuss two apparently highly self-reliant[1] participants who explain that 'myself' matters most at the moment. Charelle and Danny reflected on why and how they had come to see themselves as mattering most.

A deep sense of doubt about the future, evident for Brittany and Corrina, was also articulated even more emphatically by Danny and Charelle.[2]

Shared deliberation was surprisingly important. Mental time travel, in the contexts of multiple adversities, was key for both participants in giving an account of their particular stance toward self, society, and the future.

An embodied sense of anger – linked partly to having been bullied in school – is discussed by Charelle, and Danny recalls a depressive episode when his reflexive thoughts were "dead".

Charelle

Charelle, aged 20, is a woman in transition from care. She had spent 10 years in care, had been excluded from school and had left school at age 14. She has no qualifications but is looking for work. She has not completed any educational courses but hopes to start a course soon.

Interviewer:	So, did you have any thoughts after last week's interview?
Charelle:	Not really [laughter].
Interviewer:	OK. During this interview I would like to know about what is most important to you. So, what matters most in your life at the moment?
Charelle:	At the moment, myself. Myself obviously because I've got to think … how my rent's being paid, how I'm budgeting, I've got to think of myself at the moment 'cos I'm not working so I've got to think of where my life's going. So, myself, yeah … I'm going to college September … I'm looking into doing some volunteer work.

She then discusses her birth family and the deleterious impact of having lost meaningful emotional contact during childhood – and how much this *matters*:

'Obviously not having my mum around is always going to affect me and being in care is always going to affect me and affect how I think and feel about things, how my relationships are and everything, do you know what I mean? But that, that will always affect me, and it will affect everyone else who's around me as well.'

She includes her birth siblings[3] in her strong sense of loss of birth family contact: "Even with my brother and sister, I didn't see them [that is, services] trying to help us keep in contact, do you know what I mean?"

About her brother: "We always used to be the closest, but from then [being taken into care] there's a break in the bond. I feel it so I know he must feel it, and everyone must feel it in the family. We've all [young people in care?] got a break somewhere."

It is clear from all she says that her birth family matter to her, but they are *not* mentioned directly in her account – at the start of the second interview – of 'Which areas of your life matter most to you at the moment?' Rather it is indirectly – their importance discussed after, and separately from, the answer to the specific question about what matters.[4] As she says in relation to her birth family: "I try not to think about it."

Then Charelle discusses her hope for attending college (compare Nailah and Tyreece in Chapter 5):

> 'Well, I'm going to college in September ... I'm not really thinking ahead of that at the moment, and I don't want to as I always tell myself, "Take one step at a time"'cos I always think, the more far ahead you think about something, the less likely it is to happen.'

Charelle is clear that her primary focus must be on keeping her accommodation – her "roof over her head" – and perhaps going to college in the autumn/fall. *In those senses*, what matters is herself: "Well, if I don't have a roof over my head, I can't do anything. That is obviously my main thing 'cos I ain't got no mum, no guardian, or anyone to look after me, so if I ain't looking after me, who is?"

If one takes her two lengthy and deeply thoughtful internal conversations interviews as a whole, she spends a significant amount of time discussing her birth mother, birth siblings, and birth father. Also, her most recent foster mother – to whom she is very close, and from whom she continues to receive significant support – clearly *matters*.

She feels emotionally distant from her birth family, but they are the subject of much reflexive deliberation:

> 'You've got to protect yourself'cos nobody else is there for you. That's how it is. Like with your parents, like that's your backbone, they hold you up when you're falling and whatever. We never had that. It's only us keeping ourselves up. So when it comes to people, it's like "hold on, I'm not going to let no-one push me 'cos I've only got myself to pick myself up".'

But she is also able to use memories of her birth family to make decisions now: her choice of what to study at college is influenced by memories of positive things her birth mother said to her about her artistic abilities. And her birth father "came back into my life recently and obviously I had to think about all of the past things that happened to decide if I want to be in contact with him".

Charelle is adamant that she doesn't plan ahead, but, as we have seen, she does reflexively think about past experiences (mental time travel) in relation to current decisions: "'Cos of the life I grew up in, some things from my past affect what's happening now, so ... I have to re-think what happened then to help me decide what I'm gonna do now if that makes sense?"

Her deeply thoughtful accounts of her birth family, and of school, and of services,[5] contain reflexive accounts of her anger – anger remembered from the past. For instance, Charelle remembers (compare Nailah, Chapter 5):

> 'When I started secondary school and got bullied[6] ...
> all this other stuff added and made my temper worse
> and worse – it just exploded all the time – just the
> littlest thing from someone touching my crisps I'd go
> mad and start smashing the house – it was bad man,
> it was bad.
>
> I still have anger problems, but it's a lot better
> because I can control my anger, but I do have a bad
> temper – if I do lose it – everyone knows to keep
> away from me.'

On planning, Charelle is aware of her immediate college plans, and the potential for university, but wants to take one step at a time, and feels that "the more far ahead you think about something, the less likely it is to happen".

Using the phrase 'go with the flow', she also mentions the recent and unexpected loss of a grandparent, and how that had made her less willing to plan ahead. "And to be honest, I'm not really good with time ... I just kind of don't plan, I don't really ... a lot of the time I'm late ... I've been to the Doctor 'cos of sleep problems ... I've never had a normal routine."

The interviewer asked about 'forgetting' and planning:

> 'It's not forget. It's just that I don't really plan like that
> [planning for the following day]. I don't like planning

ahead ... other stuff comes up ... My friends know me – just 'cos I got a plan [to meet up] don't mean I'm going to come. Half the time I make a plan and don't even turn up. My friends get that and don't find it nothing bad. They're used to it.'

Danny

Danny, aged 20, is a man who had spent 3 years in residential care after a lengthy period of severe family instability. He left school at the age of 14, and has received no further 'formal' education since then. He is employed in retail.

Interviewer:	During this interview I'd like to know about what is most important to you. So, by this I mean what matters to you most in your life at the moment?
Danny:	Oh, OK, erm – what matters in my life at the moment – um, well, that's not much to go on – I only part – I really think I can come up with an answer to this myself – the only thing that matters to myself is me. Because if I let everything else – if I start mattering in things like personal relationships, family, it's all going to go wrong in the end. That's what – it *might* go wrong in the end – sorry. But I always believe that if you make yourself matter the most you always can make other people feel that they can matter to you afterwards.

In the first interview Danny had explained that:

'I had trouble when I was a child. No-one would talk to me, my parents didn't pay me any attention, stuff like that. And I never really had friends. I just had people who wanted to hang around with me to be a clown.

So, I developed a state of mind where the only person I could trust is myself and my head. And my head tells me what to do. And I believed in that all the way through my life ... I always base my decisions on that.'

Reflecting on what his own internal conversations/reflexivity offer him:

'I actually do have conversations with my actual mind ... it kind of abbreviates on what I am myself ... it's like a shorthand. That's the whole point of my basis of what I do ... using it [internal conversations] as a second person when there's no one around. Well, who helps you to your future? Yourself – your head.'

Reflecting further on his "conversations with my actual mind": "I feel like I'm my own mum. It's kind of scary ... It's weird but I don't know, it's kinda nice to know 'Danny, you can rely on yourself'. I think it's a mum role really."

Like Charelle, Danny feels emotionally distant from his birth family: "So, I know for a fact that I can't rely on my family." However, he actively remembers things his birth father said: "My dad's given me inspiration like speeches and stuff like philosophy when I was younger ... I didn't listen ... I just thought my dad was a raving looney ... but I realise [now] that there's some points my father was correct."

His family was also supportive during a recent mental health crisis/severe depressive episode, precipitated by loss of trust with friends. He had felt accused, and not wanted: "My thoughts were actually dead – my mind was silent. Everything went completely grey. It took a good three to four months. I had to take time but then I started picking myself up. My family came round and visited me and cooked my dinner."

For Danny, overcoming the depression involved: "Becoming more and more self-reliant on myself."

We discuss apparent inconsistency (family support was evident – Danny disclosed it in the interview as part of his narrative – but he regarded increased self-reliance as the key to recovery) later in this chapter.

Like Charelle, Danny didn't endorse forward planning: "'cos I don't believe in future ... like I don't believe that anything can out-beat the future, or [that] past can make your present."

In the first interview he had said (emphatically): "I don't believe in planning further ahead because you never know. You *never* know [Danny's emphasis]." And: "you can't anticipate an unknown enemy", and "I don't believe in future".

On ambitions, Danny was both reflective, and gently humorous:

> 'To be honest, no. I'm actually stumped for an ambition at the moment. How do you put it ... writer's block? ... [L]ast time I had an ambition was – to buy a cake – that was about it ... it was just a cherry cake – I just wanted a cake with cherries on top.'

The interviewer gently asked if staying depression-free might be a 'goal' and Danny replied: "Yeah, I'd say 'goal' there, I'll give you that [laughs]."

On what mattered, later in the interview, social mixing clearly was important: "having a laugh with all my friends and actually being part of the group. That makes me a good positive idea and that's what I like. And that's what makes me feel better about myself as I know people want me to come and join them."

After more discussion about the importance of social mixing:

Interviewer:	So, it sounds like – although you said at the beginning that the most important thing is yourself, it sounds like relationships are actually an important part of yourself?
Danny:	Um, well, actually it is, yeah, actually I'm contradicting my own self really, um, yeah, but it's not essential in my life – it's not an essential ... I need to be myself, to do the stuff I want to do – I like a bit of self-reliancy.

Danny's two interviews, like Charelle's, were lengthy and thoughtful. He had a deep understanding of internal conversations in the context of chronic adversity and social isolation during childhood.

Although being sociable did not figure in his response to the interview question about what matters, there were several sections of the interviews in which other people featured clearly or strongly in his thinking. First, as mentioned earlier, he values having genuine fun with friends who appreciate his presence. This matters in the sense of providing a boost to his self-worth – which he acknowledges, albeit with the understandable proviso that this must be on his terms. Second, in another part of the interviews he discusses how he has "lots of people to talk to", and "I like to listen to understand [where] he's coming from", and "I learn, I learn a lot ... from everyone else, no matter what they speak". Third, his family provided support during his severe depressive episode

Comparison

Articulating what and who matters

Charelle and Danny reflected in depth on why and how they had come to see *themselves* as mattering most. Both of them reflexively and 'seamlessly' explained to the interviewer that their self-reliant stances were linked autobiographically (mental time travel) to their experience of deeply upsetting and long-standing family ruptures and losses, and for Charelle, peer victimisation. These ruptures and losses were conceptualised and *felt* as having a semi-permanent/ongoing effect on self and on relationships (a view of the future?).

Indeed, Danny discusses the importance of reflexivity *itself* – his sense that his own mind telling him what to do provides a "safe haven in a way". His own interpretation is that his internal conversations "abbreviate" on his "own self".[7] We get a strong sense, from his interviews, of the *vital* importance – to him – of his own thoughts (and, in contrast, during his depressive episode "my thoughts were dead"). In summary, Danny not only discusses how he uses reflexivity, but also values it 'for itself', as a vital and security-providing fundamental of his day-to-day existence. He recognises that this 'second self within himself' is like a "mum role". It is necessarily self-protective, and ironically/paradoxically, is in place of an emotionally available mother.

(Contrast Brittany and Corrina, in Chapter 3, who don't find internal conversations intrinsically helpful but do value shared time and shared deliberations with others.)

Charelle, using a powerful embodied simile, also connects the importance of her self-reliance *to the lack of emotionally available parents*: "like that's your backbone, they hold you up when you're falling" and "we never had that". She talks about how the loss of deep emotional contact with her birth family "will always affect me". She connects her central priority of securing her housing accommodation by explaining: "Well, if I don't have a roof over my head, I can't do anything. That is obviously my main thing 'cos I ain't got no mum."

Anger seemed 'close to the surface' for both Charelle and Danny. More broadly, the narratives were emotional, expressive – these tonal aspects infused both participants' interviews (as was also the case with Nailah and Tyreece – Chapter 5).

Whereas Brittany and Corrina (see Chapter 3) loved the sense of shared conversations with family (and preferred this to self-talk/ internal conversations), Charelle and Danny were highly selective (and circumspect) about socialising and shared deliberation – not surprisingly, given their avowed self-reliance. But before discussing their nuanced social engagements, Charelle's commitment to her family is important to note.

Despite the long-standing family ruptures, and despite "the way I brought myself up", family still mattered to Charelle – she *cared* that her isolated and sometimes homeless birth mother, living in another part of England, appeared to be unsupported by agencies. She cared about her brothers, although she experienced a "break in a bond" with them. And it was important to her that her mother used to compliment her on her artwork as a child – a (mental time travel) memory which motivates her to aim to go to college, and helps her choose what to study (this aspect of planning).

Danny was sometimes supported by his family – for instance when he was in the middle of a mental health crisis. However, he attributed his recovery to his self-reliant internal conversations. His compounded anger with his family seemed to wipe out anything more than a description/acknowledgment of how his family had visited him and cooked meals for him, while he was experiencing a severe depression.

Danny *did* find that being with friends brought joy, and a sense of being wanted. He also says: "I have lots of people to talk to ... I like to listen to understand [where] he's coming from ... I do like to listen ... I learn, I learn a lot from everyone else, no matter what they speak."

For Charelle, socialising with friends didn't seem to matter for her – she saw herself as "an observer", vigilantly and cautiously watching and gauging other people.

But Charelle did trust certain named professionals and trusted a previous foster mother. About one professional, she says: "She'll send things, she'll tell me about work fairs [job fairs], call me – she helps me a lot actually – a lot." And about another professional: "I might talk to her [specifically] 'cos I think she know more about dot dot dot in my situation than what x [does]. I might go and talk to somebody who knows about that situation or has been through it – and say 'can you help me with this, or whatever'. It depends." One foster carer remains important: "She taught me lots of things, she did ... even to this day I speak to her every week – I spoke to her Sunday – I see her whenever I want."

Danny remembers what his Dad used to say: "He taught me life lessons in a sense – but he taught me in words, he wasn't showing me in actions."

Shared deliberation (and other aspects of social life, such as having fun with friends) was surprisingly important to Danny, and especially to Charelle, despite their avowed self-reliance.[8] As shared deliberation and shared agency are a key part of Bratman's central 'building blocks' of planning (see Chapter 8), it is of special theoretical (and practical) importance to note that both Charelle and Danny, despite avowed self-reliance, 'do' shared deliberation, as does Nailah, as we shall see in Chapter 5 (Nailah also sees herself as self-reliant, but also highly sociable).

Planning

Charelle applies her reflexive sense of what matters, her sense of self-reliant 'survival', to important *moment-to-moment decisions*, such as if a friend wants to meet up – which might cost money – and a housing bill is due, she refuses to meet up. Or, for an imminent job centre interview: "You can't just go there ... you have to think in your head 'what am I going to say' ... there's a lot of thinking to do ... everything you do you've got to think."

However, Charelle *strongly* feels that she does not plan for the near future or the far future. Her approach to the upcoming college place is not only 'step by step' but also "the more far ahead you think about something, the less likely it is to happen". In her words: "I'm not good with time."

Danny is even more emphatic about not planning ahead, and not making big decisions: "Because I don't believe in it – I don't, I don't. I don't believe in it."

As Danny says about the future: "'Cos I don't believe in future ... I don't believe that anything can out-beat the future."

Close reading and re-reading of Danny's transcript suggests a highly internally reflexive focus, with a careful and intricate (and resourceful?) tying together of thought and feeling via his own personal thoughts, and/but with little sense of how this links to day-to-day action, or future-oriented planning.

At the end of the second interview, he says: "Roll with the punches, glide through the waves, sting like a bee."

5

Time future: time complex

In the case illustrations in Chapters 3 and 4, planning agency, although usually evident on a day-to-day basis, had a relatively short future time horizon.

In the two case examples in this chapter, an avowedly self-reliant young woman (Nailah) has a reflexive sense of the future in which she discusses how her *sense of time* has been affected before and during the transition from out-of-home care, and a young man (Tyreece) articulates a complex set of what matters and who matters, with a provisional – or conditional – sense of the future.

Embodiment forms a strongly felt part of self-reflection/reflexivity for both. The social aspects of reflexivity, *including shared deliberation*, are vitally important to both.

(In these secondary analyses I ask at what point participants discussed a particular matter. Let us remember that the specific interview questions about what and who matters, and planning, occur, by design at the beginning of the *second* interview[1] after the first interview gave the participants the opportunity to flex their internal conversational/reflexive 'muscles' – and to get to know the interviewer.)

Nailah

Nailah, aged 21, is a woman in transition from care. She had been in foster care for 5 years, and had left school at the age of 15. She is a part-time student, with her own accommodation, and is looking for work.

Interviewer:	Did you have any thoughts about internal conversations afterwards [that is, after Interview 1]?
Nailah:	Yes. I did have some thoughts about that. Answering kind of those questions made me aware, made me think about, "Yeah I do do that." It's kind of a self-reflection thing.
Interviewer:	Anything else you thought you wanted to say or noticed?
Nailah:	That I focus on the future far too much. That's it (laughs) ... I think I should put less pressure on myself.

A few moments later, answering the interview question about what matters most:

'OK. First things first. Getting my education out of the way and done with 'cos I hate studying but I need to. Being financially stable ... having a part-time job ... and go really and release my stress and socialise as that's the thing I like doing the most [laughs].'

Nailah talks much about her socialising, her love of being with people, and how, although she feels "not academically smart", she *does* feel "smart ... when it comes to society, people, life and all that stuff".

She also emphasises her sense of her own mental "determination": "Like I'm very determined and proactive so – like if I want to do something I need to sort something out I think 'how am I going to do it?' – and just get up and go and do it."

Although Nailah has a strong sense of her own 'what matters', and her confidence in prioritising what matters most (and why), and her own *self-determination*, she also reflects, in the first sections of the first interview, on her "habit of thinking too much ... overanalysing". She gives a recent example and concludes "I was overthinking it too much", and goes on to give more examples, including "especially like with guys", and gives a further detailed example. Summarising, she says: "I think it's good to analyse, as I said, because it makes you more aware of things ... at the same time, because I overthink too much that does cause a lot of problems in my life … I wish I didn't think too much."

Like Charelle and Danny (see Chapter 3) and Tyreece (see Chapter 5), Nailah discusses very complex, *angry, and thoughtful* feelings about her birth family. She considers the maltreatment and neglect she experienced at home – this is raised by her straight after the 'what matters' section – and how her birth parents "really think they done nothing wrong".

> 'I hated my past and it made me … I was like I hate my situation that I'm in like at home with my Mum, actually 'No', I was just put in care. I'm not sure, I can't remember … I hated my childhood, I still do hate it and I always [said] I want this amazing adult life.'

Yet, through the anger about her birth parents, she is reflective: "Then I find out … that my parents were abused by their parents … I found out through other family members. It slipped out their mouth when they were saying something and I was like 'Oh, that makes sense'."

Currently in contact with her birth parents, she says: "No, they're not important, I just view them as a friend and that's it … you can't be disappointed if you view them as a friend. Soon as you view them as a parent all they're going to do is disappoint and upset you."

She also discusses the racist bullying (verbal bullying, relational bullying, and social exclusion) she experienced at school, and her formal exclusions from school – at about the same time as she was taken into care. She feels that "bullying made permanent damage to me and how I view myself", including both her sense of her own physical appearance, and her abilities in formal education.[2]

Education remains key for her, but her reflexive expectations of a potential future include a sense that: "My time's running out [but] I put too much pressure on myself." She also feels that "services put pressure on you", to decide "what you [will be] doing with yourself … what do you wanna do?", "'cos their manager is putting pressure on them".

Nailah, reflecting on the time leading up to leaving foster care, recalls being frightened of the approaching transition – "horribly scary" – and her fear of being homeless.[3]

She also recalls that a recent application for an educational course foundered because of a series of service-based administrative errors. The errors delayed her acceptance by the course for another whole year. She recalled, reflexively, the sense she had of each of the services' failures to appreciate *the meaning to her* of this administrative blunder, and resultant delay, in the context, for her, of an already compounded history of educational disruption, exclusion, bullying, victimisation, and self-doubt. She described the mental health issues that arose from this particular episode:

> 'What kept me going through all them bad things in my childhood was that my adulthood would be a lot better. That's what I thought [laughs]. OK my childhood is hell but adulthood will be heaven as long as I put the hard work and the effort in. I can turn it around and make my adulthood great. But I guess now I'm thinking fifty-fifty – I'm kind of a bit on the lost side.'

Tyreece

Tyreece, age 20, is a man who spent 3 years in care. He is currently attending a further educational course and an additional course, and is volunteer-working.

Answering the interview question about what matters most:

> 'There is a lot of things that's important to me right now. There's a lot. There's me wanting to finish my course ... getting my qualification ... getting my distinction; also, you know, having my people around me, my brother and my friends around me. It's important to me to have my two key friends like around, I always want them around. I know it isn't as important, but ... having a woman now, as well as those letters [the further education qualification] ... it's not the biggest concern ... but I need a female's attention in my life ... there is also the fact that I need to pay off my fine ... I need to pay off my mobile [cell-phone] provider ... but these are small stupid mistakes.'

In this dense and evocative account of what matters and who matters Tyreece reflexively sums up the many aspects of his life that he holds in mind. In the interview he follows this by outlining the structure of his very busy week – what he does each day, and how he plans – during the evening – for the following day.

But, on longer-term planning: "I don't plan too far ahead, that's one thing I've learned ... plan is good but I don't plan too far ahead because right now I'm young ... right now I'm just getting my qualifications." And "right now I see it as I am still trying, I'm still finding my way".

He is fascinated by his own internal conversations, and his imagination:

> 'I think ... I've always reasoned with myself and talked to myself ... I've learned to work well with my brain ... like I use visual, I visualise in my head – that's my way of learning and my way of thinking ... and I would be like "how can I learn to use the rest of my brain?"'

He enjoys 'clarifying' (one of the verbal prompts in the internal conversations interview), both for himself and with others: "Clarifying to me is good." He feels *appreciated* by the important others in his day-to-day life.[4] And he feels that "I got people that love me". The "two key friends" he mentions have been, from the time he had been in care, through to now, like "family":

> 'We've just been through it together ... if I had money ... I look after him ... you know, he eating, I'm eating ... that's who I saw as my family ... our little family ... I just saw them as my family as in [name], [name] and me, in and out, and I know them in and out, yeah.'

He does discuss his birth family. About his father he uses an angry expletive, then "No, my dad is not important to me at all, no". But at several different points in the two interviews – *not* in the 'Which areas of your life matter most to you at the moment?' section – he discusses the central importance of his relationship with his birth mother, a relationship which had broken down when he was taken into care, but was now 'alive' again:[5] "My [birth] mum now is cool, cause she's seen the man I've turned out to be ... and she knows the respect that I get ... she's back to my mum, my proper mum, the mum I always wanted." He sees her regularly.

Shortly after discussing what matters and "I got people that love me", he says: "I just think there is all sorts of things wrong with me." He specifies, then reflects/says:

> 'Life experience has affected me even from – basically things that have affected me in the past are affecting me today, even 'til today they are still affecting me, like my overthinking, my self-awareness that of myself, I just don't like my ... I don't know why, I just don't.'

With the interviewer's help he then discusses further his overthinking and overanalysing, and "my brain just shoots things at me". He regards this as another aspect – a much less happy aspect – of internal conversations – the tendency to overanalyse past situations that have been problematic, or challenging situations that are 'coming up'.

He also talks, in the same discussion, about his account of the origins of his 'overthinking': "I was kind of bullied ... in the sense of verbal-like ... by my whole family[6] ... they were just taking the piss so much." His family chronically teased him ("they kept doing it and doing it") about his physical appearance (he had mentioned this also in the first interview) – "they were making me feel worse about it and I used to overthink and that's when it all started". At the end of the second interview, he says: "when I consider my problems, I just get overwhelmed by emotion" (to be discussed later; and see Chapters 7 and 8). But also, at the end of the second interview: "So long as I know those I care about are OK, nothing else really matters to me."

Comparison

Articulating what/who matters

As is the case for each of the participants discussed in Chapters 3 and 4, Nailah and Tyreece gave expressive and highly committed accounts of what and who mattered in their lives at the moment. The accounts were given with focus, and without doubt. Furthermore, there were individual logics of meanings linking what and who mattered with reflexive discussions about other aspects of their lives.

Post-school education formed a reflexive focus for both young people. For Nailah, formal education was necessary, even though she (had always) disliked it. She distinguished what she saw as her own "smartness" with people, loving being with others, from formal education – but nevertheless wanted to pursue formal education. Her strongly reflexive sense of current and future subjective time was deeply connected to her wish to gain educational qualifications – and we pick up her sense of future time, and its relation to planning, later.

For Tyreece, completing his educational courses is first on his list of what matters. In addition, for him, "life is a learning experience" and, like Nailah, he values what he learns out of school as much as in the school classroom.

Tyreece's birth family are not mentioned in the main interview section of 'Which areas of your life matter most at the moment?', but his mother is clearly central to his current life: "my proper mum, the mum I always wanted." He knows and feels that he, as he is now, is given full recognition by her (see Chapter 10).

But he is so angry with his birth father that he cannot discuss him except in dismissive terms. Nailah, in a 'different psychological place', is *thoughtfully* angry when discussing her birth parents. She reframes her relationship with her parents, actively trying to minimise the hurt.

But both young people, like Charelle and Danny (see Chapter 4), are angry, and that emotion, interweaving with so much of these young people's 'lived experience', in the past and in the present, demands our attention as researchers or practitioners. We discuss this further later, and in Chapters 9 and 10.

In Chapter 2 we discussed Vandenberghe's critique of Margaret Archer's theoretical model of reflexivity and agency – in particular that the model, in foregrounding individual reflexive deliberation, seems to omit intersubjectivity, shared deliberation, shared agency.[7] The sense of the importance of being and doing – and sometimes planning – together with others. For Brittany and Corrina *family* was where thoughts and feelings were shared – this experience was what mattered, and fundamentally affected their account of 'their own' reflexivity. In Chapter 4 Danny and Charelle were not in a position to share, reflexively, with family – but *highly valued* socialising with others – being with and listening to others.

These examples of how socialising and *shared deliberation matter* in the lived experience of some young people experiencing compounded adversity seem important. What more can we discover from Nailah and Tyreece's accounts?

Nailah, in this present chapter, like Danny and Charelle, feels distanced from her family.[8] She feels a 'break' (compare Charelle, Chapter 4), and, despite thoughtful and careful reframing about "treating them as a friend" and discovering and understanding her parents' own childhood experience of maltreatment, experiences anger about her past: "I still hate my childhood."

But Nailah *does* see herself as a "people's person" and includes "socialising ... the thing I like doing the most" in her account of what matters (this is similar to Danny's experience). Being with other people is both pleasurable, in and for itself, *and* provides a reflexive sense of what she is good at: "I'm not academically smart, but I'm smart when it comes to society, people, life and all that stuff." She reflects on giving advice to others, and how it is possible to do this sensitively, considering how the other feels and thinks.

Tyreece feels deeply connected to two friends who he identifies as important to him in the 'Which areas of your life matter most to you at the moment?' section of the interview: "we've just been through it together", and "we were like family". Here there is clearly a history of shared deliberation, of sharing together what was and is important. And it continues now. This sense of having been through adversity together, while growing up, is powerfully described.

Tyreece's relationship with his mother, which he describes as "she's back to my mum, my proper mum, the mum that I've always wanted", clearly brings deep warmth to his life, but it is perhaps important that she is not mentioned in his detailed and concentrated account of 'Which areas of your life matter most to you at the moment?' Is this because she is less important than his brother and key friends (who are mentioned), or is it because she is so important that she is not 'listed'? She is first mentioned in the middle of the second interview, after the 'what matters' section, and after a brief discussion of the circumstances in which he was first taken into care. What *is* clear is the importance he attaches to the pride she shows in him, as he is now (and as *she* is now?).

Planning

Tyreece spent part of his evenings ensuring he was ready for the following day's activities. In addition, he organised his time to ensure he met his birth mother regularly.

Nailah had a strong sense that once she had made a decision about what was important, she would be "proactive" and "go and do it". However, she felt that she wasn't good at day-to-day planning – easily being drawn to spontaneous socialising instead of other scheduled activities!

The longer-term future was more complex, for both participants.

Tyreece did plan and look ahead in time, but the clear sense from his interview was that he was "still finding my way" and "plan is good but not too far ahead" (compare Charelle in Chapter 4).

Nailah, at the beginning of her second interview, just before the 'what matters' question, says: "I focus on the future far too much. That's it [laughs] – I think I should put less pressure on myself."

In reading and re-reading her interviews it became clear that this comment was linked to several other key aspects of her ongoing experience (and ongoing reflexive review of her 'lived experience'), some of which she discussed at length, and with considerable emotion.

In the first interview, on school and on post-school education, Nailah says: "I keep on thinking my time's running out." She had wanted to be in higher education at the usual age, but now, on reflection, realised: "I missed out on a lot of schooling when I was young and stuff due to all sorts." And reflecting on more recent times:

> 'I was trying to take shortcuts, let me avoid this, jump to that … [and not recognising that others] probably had [a] good academic past, do you know what I mean?
>
> I learned from it … I need to take time with things, but because I done that mistake more than once I keep

on thinking my time's running out ... I'm worried about the time running out but I understand why I shouldn't put time on things but I felt like I had to put time on things because of my situation, my living situation being in care and everything – I felt I had to put time on things.'

Continuing with Nailah's reasoning in the first interview:

'Because they like put pressure on you, like I remember when I was in care, I wasn't sure what I wanted to do ... [they said] well you need to enrol on something de-de-de, and they put pressure on you, 'cos their manager is putting pressure on them ... every young person has to be in education.'

Continuing with Nailah's own reasoning (logical in the specific sense described in Chapter 8):

'I'm really not academic ... I'm a smart person but not pen and paper wise ... I feel like I had a time scale because there's only a certain amount of time when they will help you ... the older you get the less help you will get.

I was just worried about being left in the adult world and not being prepared for it ... because the adult world is really scary, especially when you have to be in the adult world independently. It's horribly scary and I was just worried that I wasn't going to be prepared for it and I was going to be homeless ... it can be an exaggeration but at the same time it can be realistic.'

In answer to the interviewer's question: "Are you still getting help?"

'No ... that is another thing that went wrong. I was meant to be on a [named] course this September and it just went wrong – something went wrong [laughs] the application went wrong. The college's fault, not my fault, and now I'm suffering for it and I was really crying and I was down because this is my last year of getting help ... I tried my hardest to make things happen.'

Nailah explains carefully what happened, on her account, with the course application, and she concludes: "They were just like 'Oh sorry, we have put you on the waiting list and you can re-apply next year'. *That's not the point* [Nailah's emphasis]!"

Her lived experience of – and self-reflection on – this recent episode of administrative errors was in the context of her profound sense of time pressure to garner fine-tuned support, regret and anger about past educational exclusion and failure (and racist bullying victimisation), and her sense that her own self-determination had been, apparently, to no avail. She concluded: "My hope was my future – my future was my hope ... what kept me going through all them bad things in my childhood was that my adulthood would be a lot better. That's what I thought [laughs]."

6

What matters is social: friendships and social responsibility

Zavie, who is slightly older than the other participants in this study, has a deep personal commitment to his friends (compare Tyreece in Chapter 5), and to a wider cause of addressing injustice for young people in care. He is in full-time work. *Shared deliberation* with friends is clearly a cornerstone of his reflective experience.

While Joe appears 'on the surface' to be relatively non-reflexive in his thinking, his discussion of what matters has humour, irony, reflectiveness, and focus. When deliberating on what matters, he focuses on friends, and slightly less on education, and regrets that you can't get a degree in friends!

Zavie

Zavie, aged 24, is a man who had spent 10 years in care. He has a post-school education qualification, and is in full-time work.

When asked about what mattered to him most in his life, Zavie begins by saying: "Especially as a young person that grew up in care ... I want to continue my education and continue working with young people. I want to continue being active with people who are in care. Just to kind of remove the stereotypical view."

He expounds in detail where this sense of 'what matters' had originated as he discusses his own previous experience of frequent foster placement moves, frequent changes of social workers, and the importance of the "safety network" of friends: "It's a circle of building up trust and it being broken down and building up trust and being broken down again." This, he found, was something he/we "constantly talked about with our friends":

> 'I wouldn't say it was anything to do with me. I would say it's a lot to do with my friends because when you're brought up in care, your actual network, your safety network is actually your friends. Because you haven't got family, you become stronger in friendship. And I think it was just the friendship I had, watching my friends go to different families after families, my friends being told they needed to work harder in school ... and teachers actually forgetting that they are in care and that they have been through a lot, and I've had to watch ... and that's made me reflect and made me who I am now.'

He also feels that he has gradually developed a sense of "responsibility":

> 'When you're 16 ... you're intellectually underdeveloped and when you turn 21 you start realising the amount of responsibility you actually have ... and I think a lot more, I prioritise things a lot more when it comes to money, friends, meeting up with friends, being a support network for friends.'

He makes a clear distinction between planning and having responsibilities: "I don't really *plan* my future ... I want to make money but I don't actually plan, as I'm someone who believes that you don't know what's going to happen ... every day could be your last, so I'm someone who just lives for each day." And he adds: "For me, I would say it's too hard to think about the future."

But, in contrast, on 'responsibilities' for friends: "I feel very responsible in making sure that they are OK every day if that means ringing them or emailing them."

The graduate public service job he holds was chosen partly because of the highly social aspects of it: "I meet new people ... and a diverse community of people so that's mainly why I picked this job." He sees his work as driven by both his sociable persona and his engagement with social justice: "My goals are around justice and social care and community ... I would say they are my main goals. I would say that community comes up the most just because of who I am with people and just giving to people."

Zavie is happy to use the word 'goals', not in a specific 'planning for the future' context – see earlier on his sense that he doesn't really 'plan' his future – but rather in the sense of his values and his social identity.

He loves the spontaneous enjoyment of being with friends, but also the opportunity friends provide to talk difficult things over. In the contexts of feeling confused about something that may have happened in his life:

> 'Normally that's when I would go and talk to someone else ... I tell them both sides of the – I'm a very objective person and my friends are very objective, so I tell them both sides and they see it from both points of view. And then, although the truth hurts, sometimes someone telling you back – can actually help you a lot.'

Joe

Joe, aged 19, is a man who had spent 1 year in care, is currently on an educational course, and is looking for work.

Technically, using Margaret Archer's account of fractured reflexivity, Joe's interview transcript would satisfy most of the criteria for fractured reflexivity:[1] very 'thin', brief responses to internal conversation prompts in the first parts of the interview, seeming Archerian agential 'passivity', and little narrative evidence of 'instrumental orientation'. His internal conversations might *seem* to be, again using Archer's account, 'near non-reflexive', like 17-year-old 'Jason', also a care-leaver, whom Archer interviewed in her first empirical internal conversations study.[2]

But, on careful reading and re-reading of Joe's 'Which areas of your life matter most to you at the moment?' interview section, one can see clear aspects of self-reflection, focus, and humour, especially when compared with the very spare narrative in other parts of his interview. He 'warms'[3] to the question of what matters in his life: "Hmmm ... games, hanging around with people I'd say, couple of friends … I'd say work but I'm not working yet, but I would like to … [I'm] doing a bit of studying. That's a little bit important really."

Asked by the interviewer to say which is most important:

> 'Err. Just hanging around with friends really – that's more important. Well, I know education's supposed to be more important than friends, but still … I would say education is second … and then games. I can't believe I'm actually saying it third 'cos I do like a good game.'

He says just a little bit more about education:

> 'When I was in my last college … I started to fail … I knew college was important 'cos I knew if I wanna do something else I need to pass, which I have done … *whee hee for me* … so I maybe could do another course. Even if my qualifications are shit in high school at least I got a pass in college … 'bout it really.'

And he says a little bit more about friends:

Joe:	Hmmm, well friends are quite important 'cos if you need help with something, you got no friends, then what can you do? You have friends, you need something done, then you can ask for help … concerning making friends I'm alright at that.
Interviewer:	How long have you known [your particular friends]?
Joe:	Oh, since high school – quite a few years now.

Joe comments further on friends and college: "I know that college is more important than friends, 'cos you can't really get a degree in friends … so I would say college and friends is like a half–half thing."

Although Joe's responses to internal conversation prompts were, on the whole, 'thin', one of the prompts is 'imagining', to which Joe responds as follows:

'Ah! I have a very good imagination – well, I used to, I believe, 'cos, when I was younger, I used to write stories and stuff. Actually, I did like – I wrote like half a story 'bout a year ago and never finished it – now I lost it for some reason ... and I can't remember what words I put.'

And he adds: "Well, if I'm like drawing, I'm more aware of my imagination."

Joe is clear that he doesn't plan:

Joe:	Not a very good planner. Not really much of a planner myself. I just like to go along the way it goes day by day ... I plan on the actual day itself.
Interviewer:	What about long term plans?
Joe:	No, not my style. Plus, if I did, it's either I'll forget about it, or I just can't be bothered to remember. But if I'm going somewhere on the weekend then obviously, I'll plan what to – err I'll plan what I have to do.

Joe didn't discuss family or foster family, and he expressed no 'negative feelings' in the interview.

Comparison

Articulating what/who matters

Zavie uses the 'Which areas of your life matter most to you at the moment?' section of the interview to tell how his experiences of having been in care inform his priorities to continue his education and continue working with young people, and work against the racist and social discrimination many young people in care experience. He reflexively connects these values with a long-term friendship group: "watching my friends go to different families after families ... being told they need to work harder in class ... teachers actually forgetting that they are in care ... I've had to grow up watching and that's made me reflect – that's made me who I am now." (Compare Tyreece's account of his long-term friendship group: Chapter 5.)

Seemingly highly reflective, Zavie discusses how he uses his thought processes to prioritise, make decisions, and know when to discuss complex dilemmas with friends whose judgements he trusts.

He identifies the word 'responsibilities' positively – he names "going to work, paying your bills, making sure you cook and eat, talking to your friends and making sure your friends are OK".

Joe also articulates what matters to him, and again friends are clearly important. With help from the research interviewer, he gradually unpacks what is important, and does this with gentle (reflexive) humour.

Gently self-mocking humour and irony characterise Joe's narrative. (Compare Danny's in Chapter 4.)

Zavie and Joe value friends. Both discuss friends in detail. Joe finds friends central to his sense of what, and who, matters. He is detailed on friends, relative to other parts of his interview, especially in terms of re-iteration and reflective thought. There is a suggestion that he values in particular his ability to make and sustain friendships.

Zavie – and Tyreece (see Chapter 5) – identify their own long-term friendship groups who have shared support, shared discussion, and have shared the development of a social identity of having been in care and having strongly felt views on social justice for young people in care. We return to this friendship experience, valued hugely, highly reflexive, and shared over long or significant periods of time, in Chapter 8 (shared deliberation/ shared agency as one core aspect of planning agency).

Zavie sees himself as helping others engage in shared deliberation around difficult-to-resolve matters. He gives an example of differences of views between friends of his who are "gay" and those who are "straight":

> 'I'm stuck in the middle and I try to see the point of view of my gay friends and the point of view of my straight friends and understanding that they don't like being called homophobic names and being laughed at by my straight friends and I'm also trying to understand that my straight friends are totally new to the situation and that they feel uncomfortable about being around

gay friends … weighing it up, just being in the middle
… I know that if I wasn't there, there would have
been hell.'

Planning

Zavie's sense of 'responsibility' affects his day-to-day and week-
to-week planning. In the first internal conversations section of
the interview:

> 'In your head you're thinking about things – it could
> be things that you want to do the next day, things that
> you want to do in a week's time … I don't think you
> can say it's a voice … I'd say it's thoughts – which help
> me to – um – plan.'

He explains that "if it's a more serious thing I do it [internal
conversations] more … I think in my job I realise it most …
I have a certain responsibility". But, in contrast: "I don't really
plan my future … I don't actually plan as I'm someone who
believes that you don't know what's going to happen – every day
could be your last."

Interviewer: Do you see any projects in the future?
Zavie: I would say not. Only time will tell … I would
                say it is too hard to think about the future.

His sense of his responsibilities, and the central importance of
friends, and of social justice do, however, give him "goals": "It's
about justice and my goals are around justice and social care and
community – my main goals."

Goals, for Zavie, are not future-time-oriented, or highly
specific. Rather, they are intrinsic to his sense of his personal
and social identity, and "staying true to myself": "Let's just
say I'm part of the culture – being accepting of my culture …
I have an issue … of people stereotyping black people as
being criminals."

Joe 'does not do' future-oriented planning: "Not really
much of a planner myself." However, he acknowledges

day-to-day ordinary planning, for instance if he is meeting up with friends! He also, as part of the initial interview on internal conversations, identifies imagination as something he values, and he recalls having written and drawn from his creative imagination.

7

A bridging chapter: toward a three-aspects approach to planning

Throughout Chapters 3–6 our view of the nature and scope of planning may be challenged by what (some) young people transitioning from care say about their own lives. Perhaps we might agree with philosopher Charles Taylor when he says, in the context of considering the nature of human agency: 'The centre of gravity thus shifts in our interpretation of the personal capacities. *The centre is no longer the power to plan, but rather the openness to certain matters of significance. This is now what is essential to personal agency*' (Taylor, 1985, p 105, emphasis added).

And, of course this applies both to participants and researchers/ practitioners. The double hermeneutic of qualitative research – with which we began Chapter 2 of this book – the reflexive voices of the young people *and* the reflexive meaning-making of the researchers (mirrored in practice settings – the client attempting to make sense of her own experience, *and* the practitioner making sense of the client's own meaning-making, both in the contexts of their own histories and structural and cultural contexts) is also central to this chapter and those following.

The double hermeneutic involves iteration as a "deeply reflexive process",[1] involving active meaning-making, that is, the participant repeatedly and reflexively trying to make sense of things that have happened in her life, and their implications for her future, with the researcher, equally, visiting and revisiting things discussed with the individual participant, and visiting and revisiting relevant theory.

One of the major researcher iterations of this book has been the gradual decision to focus on three aspects of planning. As I discussed in the Introduction, and Chapter 1, this journey began with internal conversations and reflexivity, seen as 'mediators' between agency and structure. It continued in Chapter 2 with a broadening of the range of possible forms of reflexivity, and the design of a secondary analysis of Hung and Appleton's qualitative data, aimed at understanding more about how young people *articulated* what matters, and how they formulated a position on planning.

Two potential aspects of planning – (a) what matters and who matters, and (b) scepticism about future planning – were already clear from our data with care-experienced young people. A third – (c) shared deliberation and shared planning – was 'robustly' present in the secondary analysis data reported in Chapters 3–6. This third aspect, though, did not 'emerge' from the data.[2] Michael Bratman's 'remarkable trio' theoretical framework of planning 'robustly' included shared agency/shared deliberation, alongside cross-temporal aspects of planning, and self-governed intentional agency (which includes "the idea that certain plan states … concern *what matters* in the sense of having weight in our deliberative thought"[3]).

I will temporarily stop here – mid-iteration. This chapter, *together with the next*, provides a 'live' iteration in which I first summarise data from Chapters 3–6 (in the three categories discussed earlier), and then, in Chapter 8, I discuss the work of Michael Bratman – a leading theorist on planning – whose work interplays in a deeply fascinating way with the narratives of the young people in Chapters 3–6. His idea of the 'remarkable trio of capacities' for planning is a major source of the idea of the three aspects model of planning for this book.

Let us hold onto the range of different voices among the eight young people. The range is extraordinary. I will summarise under the categories of the three aspects of planning: to repeat, two of which have been with us in various guises since the start of the book – what/who matters, and time and planning (initially as scepticism about future-oriented planning) – and the third, shared deliberation and shared planning which are strongly present in the secondary analysis in Chapters 3–6.

What matters and who matters

In Chapter 3, Brittany and Corrina express how much they enjoy spending time with family. Brittany looks forward each week to caring for her foster nieces and nephews. Corrina imagines what her loved paternal grandfather might have said about her father, when he, her birth father, wishes to re-join the family he left. Corrina trusts her foster family – and a key worker – to help her deal with mental health issues that might arise 'at any moment'. For both participants, family is a 'special place' where feelings and thoughts can be shared, where there is a common ground – or potential common ground – of feeling and experience (and *also* conflicted feelings). Brittany values her new accommodation and her sense of self-governance about this, comparing it in detail (mental time travel) with her previous housing experience. Corrina expects to go to college soon, but does not feel able to forward plan for this.

In Chapter 4, Charelle and Danny poignantly discuss their sense of distance from their birth families – Charelle employing the embodied metaphor of how a family should provide a 'backbone' of support. Danny finds vital support in his own thoughtfully described reflexivity but acknowledges that this – his own, avowed, self-protective, and self-reflective thinking – might fulfil "a mum's role". Despite family estrangement, Charelle cares deeply about her highly vulnerable birth mother. And despite seemingly absolute self-reliance, Danny looks forward to being with friends, having fun, or listening to what friends say. Both young people express anger about loss of family ties.

In Chapter 5, Tyreece expresses deep closeness to friends who "have been through it together", and Nailah loves being with other people and feeling 'people-person-smart' with friends, despite her huge struggles to take formal education forward. Tyreece feels close again to his birth mother, "the mum I always wanted", but is so angry with his father he is unable to express this in words (except via swearing). Nailah, also angry with the birth family who maltreated her, is back in touch with them, and has found a way to lower her expectations of their company. Nailah also discloses chronic bodily effects (and affects) of adolescent racist bullying victimisation. Time, and good use of time, has mattered for Nailah. Her reflections on this, and how time and planning interweave, is discussed later.

In Chapter 6, neither of the young men discuss family, but do place great value on friendships, Zavie regarding his friends as almost inseparable from his sense of himself and his sense of "responsibility" – a word he prefers to goals. Joe realises, in discussion about what matters and who matters, that friends are probably more important to him than education and, tongue-in-cheek, says he realises you can't get a degree in friends.

A sense of personal time

Scepticism about future-oriented planning is strongly expressed, and there is a web of reasons and personal logic which each participant proactively discusses. The expressive thoughts and feelings – about planning for the future – varied from outright antipathy to thoughtful and active avoidance.[4] Active mental time travel to the past was strongly evident for all participants. Short-term planning and day-to-day organisation of life seems evident for most participants.[5] A set of *reflexive* reasons – a personal logic, specific to each participant – is given for not wishing to future-plan.

For Corrina, in Chapter 3, scepticism about planning included both her previous experience of "things not working out" and current, day-to-day mental health issues. For Brittany it is the recent loss of a loved family member. Brittany talks in depth about her nieces and nephews mattering, but she also *organises* to get a bus each week to their house. And she identifies her new flat/accommodation as mattering, but this also means *ensuring* she has enough money to pay for it, and she tries to make it nice by buying pretty things for it.

In Chapter 4, Charelle's sense that the further ahead you think the less helpful it is (and "I am not good with time") is compared with Danny's apparently comprehensive sense of picturing the future: "I don't believe in it."

In Chapter 5, Tyreece's sense that he is still finding a way is compared to Nailah's "deep doubts" about her own sense of the future, and her very complex idiographically explained and philosophical sense of time and planning. Tyreece makes sure he sees his birth mum regularly, and explains how he takes time in an evening to plan the next day.

In Chapter 6, Zavie's expressive account that every day could be your last (recall that Zavie successfully holds down a full-time graduate job) is linked to his own sense of "responsibilities", which entail keeping in close touch with friends to make sure they are OK. Joe discusses how he simply doesn't do forward planning, but does day-to-day ordinary planning,

The complex of sometimes strong emotion about future-oriented planning, and linked autobiographical logic led to ('self-reflexive') irony for some participants:[6] Danny's ambition for a (cherry) cake, and his allowing discussion about some "goals"; Zavie allowing discussion about goals almost to please the interviewer, and discussing his seriously and strongly held sense of responsibility as an alternative to future-oriented planning or goals.

Shared deliberation and shared planning

Shared deliberation (see Chapter 2) was discussed by the majority of participants, even though the internal conversations interview did not specifically prompt discussion on intersubjective aspects of thinking, feeling, or planning.

Even the most seemingly self-reliant participants – Charelle and Danny (Chapter 4), and Nailah (Chapter 5) – discussed shared deliberations, Charelle with a foster carer, Danny with friends, and Nailah with friends. In addition, Charelle and Nailah discussed individual trusted professionals with whom they felt they could discuss matters. While this seemed to 'go against the grain' of their avowed self-reliance, close reading of the interview transcripts showed individual logics for the value placed on sharing ideas and having fun together, while also remaining self-reliant.[7]

In Chapter 3, Corrina and Brittany emphasise shared deliberation, both experiencing shared history and a 'common ground' with family. Corrina extends her family-based shared deliberation to the imaginative incorporation of the voice of a deceased grandfather.

In Chapter 5, Tyreece's long-term shared history of joint commitment and joint discussions with two particular friends continues, as it does for Zavie in Chapter 6. For Zavie, the availability of friends to check out complex social matters is also highly valued.

Importantly, we might bear in mind the disrespect,[8] and the profound ruptures of shared deliberations and shared time that each of the participants experienced during childhood, adolescence, and emerging adulthood in relation to family (including siblings), friends, and professionals. So, these current, active, *positive experiences* of shared deliberation and shared agency are surely important, not only as 'social support', but also as 'material components' of planning, as "indispensable to explaining social outcomes",[9] and as personal examples of potential recognition.[10]

Three aspects of planning as strengths

The three aspects might *each* be viewed as strengths, in contrast to the view that a lack of future-oriented planning might be regarded as a vulnerability.

In Chapter 8 we discuss each aspect in considerable detail.

8

From reflexivities to planning: the 'remarkable trio' of Michael Bratman

> They arrive, we are amazed and holding our breath as the large travel cases open to reveal smaller cases and yet smaller cases until the whole space is filled with cases. We see FIVE different colors of cases with various markings, numbers, names, stickers from other concert sites, airline cargo markings, train stickers, and other nondescript sign-symbols.
>
> Joseph Jarman, liner notes to Art Ensemble of Chicago, *Urban Bushmen*, ECM, 1982[1]

With this 'kaleidoscopic scene'[2] portrayed by jazz musician Joseph Jarman in mind, each participant's research interview transcript seems metaphorically like this – each re-reading throwing more and different light on the individual young person's own expressively interwoven logic about what matters, who matters (and how and why), shared deliberation, and planning.

Michael Bratman's theoretical model also seems like this, with each re-reading (and with each re-reading of critiques of, and alternatives to, the model) throwing more and sometimes entirely different light on how we might think about planning.

There are three parts to this chapter: first, Bratman's 'remarkable trio' model of planning; second, a critique and reformulation of one aspect of Bratman's model – the cross-temporal aspect; and third, an outline of the notion of what we might mean by an individual, personal, autobiographical, 'expressively interwoven' logic for planning.

Michael Bratman's account of planning agency: the remarkable trio

In 2013, US philosopher Michael Bratman published a paper, 'The fecundity of planning agency'.[3] It summarised several years of deeply fascinating and influential work on the philosophy of planning agency.[4] Although we will need to take issue with aspects of Bratman's work – in particular via the creative interplay between Bratman's ideas and the voices of young care-leavers – it does give us more than a head start in thinking about planning (completely) differently.

In his 2013 paper, Bratman suggests that planning agency involves a 'remarkable trio of capacities': self-governance, shared planning, and temporally extended agency. I will discuss self-governance first – although re-reading this, and re-reading some of Bratman's works, and re-reading Chapters 3–6 – suggests that there should be no fixed linear order for the 'remarkable trio'.

Self-governance, what matters, and planning

> My proposal is that a key to a ... model of our self-governance is the idea that certain plan-states both concern what matters in the sense of having weight in our deliberative thought, and when functioning properly tie together our thought and action in relevant ways, both synchronically and diachronically.
>
> Michael Bratman, 'The fecundity of planning agency', 2013[5]

This excerpt is dense, so let us take time unpacking it, bearing in mind perhaps that one basic aspect of our work with transition-from-out-of-home-care clients is, as far as possible, to facilitate a client's self-governance, whether, for instance, in post-school education, overall transition planning, mental or physical healthcare, or justice.[6]

First, by self-governance we might mean the sense a person has – in some areas of her life – of having at least some (reflexive) control over her own thoughts and actions. Bratman is more specific: 'What is self-governance? As an initial, basic step we can say that in self-governance the agent herself directs and governs her practical thought and action.'[7]

Second, for Bratman, *certain plan-states concern what matters in the sense of having weight in our deliberative thought.* Chapters 3–6 carry many detailed examples of participants' thoughtful accounts of what matters. Bratman argues that these may be regarded as 'plan-states', or 'plan-like commitments to weights in deliberation'.

This is one of the core ideas for this book, that is, that planning agency is already implied and embedded in the young person's sense of what matters, or who matters, or what and who is judged to be currently most important in her life.

But what might Bratman mean by 'having weight' in our deliberative thought? In a sense we have discovered this already in the expressive detail of the young people's accounts in Chapters 3–6, and in the ideas first discussed in Chapters 1 and 2. Reflexivity, as Margaret Archer suggests, gives depth or weight to planning.[8] Plan-like commitments to weights in deliberation, at the very least, involve a 'singular-first-personal reflexivity'.[9] And if, as discussed in Chapter 2, reflexivity is to be regarded as multifaceted[10] – self-reflective, embodied, shared (sometimes), and actively involving mental time travel – then any or all of these may be taken to mean 'weight in deliberation'. The *weight* is important. Weight perhaps considered in yet more senses? Weight of expressive articulation as the young person finds words and active memories that sum up the importance of something or someone. Weight of personal logic (see later in this chapter) as an intricately connected chain of thoughts, feelings, and ideas that link the precise 'what or who matters' to an often dense web of autobiographical experience and interpretation, set in real life. Weight as psychological work-in-progress (sometimes involving 'heavy-lifting'!?), with articulations perhaps conflicted or inconsistent or contradictory within the interview, but perhaps open to discussion and clarification. Weight as imagination about matters that are important to us, including, for instance, imagining or re-imagining the voice of someone who is important to us, living or having passed,[11] or distant, or estranged. Weight as light, ironic, reflexive humour;[12] as a many-layered self-reflection. Weight as a commitment to creating and expressing something in a particular and unique way (see Lemn Sissay's teenage poems as 'flags in the mountainside';[13] and see Chapter 10 of this book).

Third, plan-states *tie together our thought and action in relevant ways.* Brittany (Chapter 3) organises her day-to-day and week-to-week life around travelling, on an agreed schedule, to care for her foster nieces and nephews. She also discusses looking after her new accommodation – payments, upkeep, and so on; but, we note, she strongly rejects future-oriented planning. (Bratman also says about this 'tying together thought and action' aspect of planning, 'when functioning properly', and I will come back to this.)

This third point, that is, that the young person's sense of what matters, or who matters, ties together thought and action – at least in the short term, at least usually holding things together day to day and perhaps week to week – is *another one of the core ideas for this book*. Bratman's account is immensely helpful in reminding us that our model of self-governance might include this 'ordinary' day-to-day (synchronic) life organisation:[14] catching the bus to visit a loved previous foster mother; turning out to meet with friends; paying a bill – on the grounds of what matters.

Which brings us to the fourth point.

On Bratman's account, plan-states work both for the short-term (Brittany's day-to-day, week-to-week coordination[15]), and for future-oriented thinking (diachronically: regarded with scepticism by the participants discussed in Chapters 3–6). As we shall see later in this chapter, it is helpful, or even central for our purposes, to unpack these two temporal aspects,[16] and/or consider a continuum of temporal horizons, and/or consider alternative temporalities – completely different ways of envisaging time. But crucially, in the short-term, Brittany seems to organise time for what and who matters, but doesn't wish to plan for the future. And Nailah's intricate account of time invites us to think very carefully indeed about what subjective time might entail for young people experiencing compounded adversity.

This first – 'what matters' and self-governance – part of Bratman's model contains a very rich hoard of ideas, ideas which connect, via reflexivities, to Margaret Archer's model of what matters (see Chapters 1 and 2) and to care-experienced young people's accounts of what matters and who matters (Chapters 3–7). What is the second aspect of planning agency?

Shared agency: social aspects of planning

> Human beings act together in characteristic ways, and these forms of shared activity matter to us a great deal. They matter to us intrinsically: think of friendship and love, singing duets, dancing together, and the joys of conversation.
>
> Michael Bratman, *Shared Agency: A Planning Theory of Acting Together*, 2014b[17]

Bratman's second aspect of human planning agency – shared, social agency – is regarded as of equal importance to that of self-governance. It is defined as: 'acting together with others in ways that go significantly beyond standard forms of strategic interaction' – *shared* planning or planning together with others. Examples he gives include painting a house together, dancing together, playing a quartet together, having a conversation together, or performing an experiment together.[18]

As with self-governance, we will take time to unpack Bratman's account of shared agency, bearing in mind perhaps that *another* basic aspect of practitioners' work with clients may be, as far as possible, to facilitate shared-governance – shared thinking and planning with others who are important to the individual young person. (And, where possible, and where appropriate, shared governance and/or co-design/co-production between practitioner and client?[19])

A young person might speak with a previous foster mother about potential housing accommodation, then visit the accommodation together, with the shared knowledge/common ground that the foster mother would have the young person's safety and security in mind.

Let us take another example. A care-leaver meets regularly in the pub with a group of friends who are also care-leavers, and with whom he has a long-standing shared bond.[20] They compare notes on a regular basis, as they have for a number of years, as well as have fun. One aspect of their regular discussion over the years is that of how care-leavers are seen by mainstream society. They recall the low expectations of some teachers and share their recall of how they tried to overcome these discriminatory events. These regular get-togethers *matter* for the young person we have in mind (see Chapters 5 and 6); they involve shared deliberation, and they involve shared planning. As in self-governing agency, reflexivity is central in Bratman's account of shared agency. In shared agency there is indeed a sense of first-person reflexivity, but here, in addition, there is a *plural* reflexive aspect[21] – as Zavie says about his friends:

> 'I wouldn't say it was anything to do with me. I would say it's a lot to do with my friends because when you're brought up in care, your actual network, your safety network is actually your friends. Because you haven't got family, you become stronger in friendship. And I think it was just the friendship I had, watching my friends go to different families after families, my friends being told they needed to work harder in school ... and teachers actually forgetting that they are in care and that they have been through a lot, and I've had to watch ... and that's made me reflect and made me who I am now.'

In Bratman's terms, Zavie is being 'doubly reflexive'[22] – referring both to his own ideas and to the fact that these ideas grew in collaboration and in shared reflective experience with friends – friends who matter.

In fact, Bratman's account of sociality might be of particular interest in the contexts of compounded adversity. It does not 'leap' straight into complex social relationships (in the way that much of clinical psychology, systemic therapy, and psychoanalysis do). Instead, the model focuses on day-to-day meaningful social cooperation with people with whom we have common ground, for example friends we have known a long time, a practitioner we trust,[23] or a trusted previous foster mother.

Let us note how much potential weight and depth *this rich ground of shared sociality* might hold, for example Zavie and his shared identity of care-experienced young people, Nailah's reframing of her relationships with her birth family, or Danny's enjoying listening to what others say.

Shared planning and shared deliberation seem to go hand in hand (see chapter 7, 'Shared deliberation, common ground', in Bratman's 2014 book *Shared Agency*). Bratman identifies three aspects of shared deliberation (coloured boxes within coloured boxes).

First, a particular shared deliberation is embedded in a *history of ongoing* shared cooperative activity by the dyad or group. This is not a one-off discussion with a stranger: the young care-leaver trusts her foster mother, and the friendship groups described by young people have shared and supported each other 'through thick and thin'.[24]

Second, shared deliberation (talking about the proposed accommodation, or talking about perceptions of care-leavers) is important *in itself* for the pair, or for the group – it *matters*. And it is potentially *planful*, and, importantly, it may lead to a *shared* plan. It is 'not just a conversation'; it is what Bratman calls a 'shared intentional activity' by the participants.

Third, there is a *common ground* of "shared commitments to treating certain considerations as mattering in our shared deliberation".[25] The care-leaver knows that her previous foster mother will want to discuss safety of the accommodation, and this matters to the young person. The friendship group shares a valuing of the experience of having been in care and having experienced the discriminatory views of some people. These shared experiences *matter*. And, crucially, some of the often complex content (of the shared common ground and shared intentions) can be tacit or implicit.[26] We come back to this later.

Summarising so far, planning is seen, on Bratman's account, as self-governance – what matters and who matters as *plan-states or plan-like commitments* – and as shared agency – acting and deliberating socially together with others in ways that 'involve distinctive forms of commitment and responsiveness to the joint activity'.

What is Bratman's third aspect?

Cross-temporal aspects of planning agency

> We are planning agents; our agency extends over time;
> and, sometimes at least, we govern our own actions.
> Michael Bratman, *Structures of Agency*, 2007[27]

Here Bratman links the first aspect, self-governance, with the third, our capacity, as human beings, of 'acting over time in ways that involve important forms of intentional cross-temporal organization and coordination'.[28]

This third Bratmanian aspect is fundamental to his thinking about how we, as humans, organise our intentions and settle future courses of action. For example, at the beginning of his 2013 paper, Bratman takes 'growing vegetables in your garden' as portraying the cross-temporal organisational aspect of planning agency. Over time, he says: 'you need to prepare the soil, plant, water, cultivate, and harvest.'[29] The example is straightforward – perhaps. There is preparatory work, then there is relevant action, then we must cultivate or support our actions, then we harvest the results of our work. Bratman emphasises the gardener's practical commitment. This 'gardening business' is not just a weighty, reflexive, deliberative 'idea' in her head – she is *committed*, in a practical, day-to-day sense, to the (future-oriented) activities that initiate and support growing vegetables in her *real-world garden*. To use Margaret Archer's phrase, she decides what 'courses of action' are required.

He also emphasises what he calls the *mind-infused* aspects of her practical planning,[30] contrasting this with the 'biological organization of seeds developing into beans'. Our minds allow us – reflexively – to imagine a whole range of things we may need to do to make the garden happen. And our minds allow us to dovetail (Margaret Archer's word) our actions in support of each other in space and time; each of the actions matter. In his garden-variety (his words) example of planning, Bratman notes that the activities 'take place over time, and that each of them is infused with the agent's understanding of and commitment to the larger temporally extended arc of the activity'.[31] We can picture this temporally extended aspect of planning both for short-term aspects (finding a spade to dig) and longer-term aspects (regular care for the growing plants). We can also picture the importance of the gardener's grasp of several interconnected and organisational aspects of the project 'going forward', and her commitment to the project as a whole. And – to connect to the first part of Bratman's remarkable trio – this garden 'matters'.

The cross-temporal aspect of human agency provides a deep root of Bratman's model. He argues that our partial, revisable, time-organised, plans 'provide a background framework for downstream thought and action'.[32]

Furthermore, for Bratman, such future-time-sensitive plans 'involve the (implicit) acceptance of and guidance by rationality norms of stability, coherence, and consistency'.[33] Such guidance (self-guidance) by rationality norms is profoundly part of Bratman's model of planning. However, this aspect is contentious for some scholarly commentators,[34] and it has given much pause for thought for a model we are considering for its relevance to some young people who are deeply sceptical about forward planning (that is, a fundamental questioning of so-called rationality norms). Furthermore, what about the long temporal haul of 'processing' and potentially healing the experiential ruptures of repeated violations of norms by significant others during the formative years of childhood and adolescence?[35]

Of course, some young care-experienced people *do* willingly forward plan, and presumably accept and use rationality norms in order practically to achieve future ends such as going to – and staying at – university, while also 'processing' complex and repeated autobiographical emotion ruptures.

But our subjective time moves in many directions. Not only forward, but also backwards, as we saw repeatedly in the young people's narratives, and as we discussed in the section on mental time travel in Chapter 2. To quote Bratman: 'This plan-based cross-temporal organization normally involves both future-looking and past-looking cross-temporal referential connections.'[36]

Our focus on mental time travel in Chapter 2, and then in each of the case-based chapters, provides many examples of cross-temporal thinking about how (recalled) real-world events in the past are actively related by the planning agent to what matters in the present.

As for the future, there is of course a very complex story to tell about how some young people transitioning from care view the future – while also reviewing the past. I discuss this next.

Cross-temporal planning – under conditions of compounded adversity

Preamble

We might note that Michael Bratman's gardener is fortunate. She has a garden space, or perhaps has access to an allotment/ community garden. She is in a position to obtain seeds or plants. She has access to water, or will need actively to search for water. Let us also note that some gardeners may have had a previous garden, or gardens, removed or destroyed. This will likely affect how they think and feel about planning a new garden. And, for the new garden, whether in the backyard or in an allotment/ community garden, what is the quality of the soil, and how much previous growth, or dumped rubble, needs clearing away?

Introduction

As discussed in detail in Chapters 1–7, *some* young adults in transition from out-of-home care are sceptical about planning for the future. In the terms of Michael Bratman's theoretical framework of planning agency, such scepticism would seem – on the surface – to undermine one key aspect of planning, that is, temporally extended, diachronic, forward-looking, or even future-embracing[37] cross-temporal intentional agency. Considering cross-temporal planning as a whole, such scepticism would appear to undermine *one crucial if not fundamental aspect* of cross-temporal planning, that is, the longer-term, future arc of cross-temporal planning. However, two other (Bratmanian) aspects of cross-temporal planning seem to be 'in place' for the young people discussed in Chapters 3–6 – active autobiographical memory for past experiences, actively and vocally recalled to connect with current accounts of what matters and who matters, *and* various degrees of short-term coordination of day-to-day and perhaps week-to-week life (tying together thought and action in the short-to-medium term).[38]

By decomposing Bratman's cross-temporal aspects of planning we are able to see two potential 'strengths' (autobiographical memory and short-term planning/life organisation),[39] while also able to focus more precisely on the – equally strong – aspect of scepticism about future planning.

But, we might say, the future arc is what matters – it is *the point* of mental time travel, it is the point of reviewing the past. So how might we understand young people's sceptical and thoughtful and expressive positions/logics about future-oriented planning? This is a central question for this book.

I address the question in three ways:

1. Through Bratman's own recognition of the possibility of a range of modes of self-governance and planning: 'For all that I have said, there may be a plurality of modes of reflective, anchored deliberation and autonomy ... in theorizing about human autonomy we should not assume, without argument, that it may not come in different forms.'[40] An example of the need for a plurality of modes starts with a critique by several scholars *of the assumption of a stable lifeworld* in that aspect of Bratman's model that deals with cross-temporal and future-oriented planning.

2. By considering an account of the impact of interpersonal trauma and post-traumatic stress disorder (PTSD) on a '*sense of foreshortened future*'[41] (see Chapter 9 for more on this).

3. By looking into the notions of alternative, crip, and queer temporalities – a literature that may help readers (and this author) *jump right out* of the usual range of subjective time thinking (and certainly out of the part of the Bratman planning model that envisages time in a standard, if beautifully cross-referential way), and more into *completely different* and reflexive and embodied and performative and expressive time-spaces, thereby beginning to open up a way of thinking about *alternative temporalities for some care-leavers*. Scepticism about the future, and planning for the future, would be just one alternative temporality, itself having many different aspects or forms.[42]

A plurality of modes of planning, which Bratman acknowledges, and two critiques

Bratman, while addressing a critique of his planning agency model by Elijah Millgram,[43] a critique that raises the question of what to do if the world changes in fundamental ways that make your prior plans and policies inapt or pointless, acknowledges:

> Although I have emphasized a kind of temporally extended self-governance that involves stability of commitment over time, I fully agree that such extreme cases [he refers to Millgram's examples of impossible-to-anticipate changes in a person's life circumstances] call for basic change and that arriving at such basic change can be an important form of self-governance.[44]

Millgram, in a paper entitled 'Segmented agency', notes that 'Bratmanian [planning] policies can be suitable guides for actions within a stable niche ... in well-structured and well-understood environments'.[45] Millgram, in arguing for a different model of planning agency,[46] emphasises that in understanding human planning we will need to understand the extraordinary variability of environments, and understand how humans are equipped to inhabit much more variable environments than some other species.[47]

Philosopher Jennifer Morton[48] also focuses on 'ecological' aspects of planning rationality, drawing attention to 'the role the environment can play in determining what norms we should use in practical deliberation',[49] and the role of the psychology of the particular agent. For Morton, 'the norms that should structure deliberation are those that enable an agent with a particular psychology in a particular environment to deliberate so that she ends up doing what she has most reason to do'.[50]

A sense of a foreshortened future

On the matter of time, philosopher Matthew Ratcliffe wryly notes: 'The acknowledgement that there are different *ways of being in time*, involving different experiences of transition [between past, present, and future], complicates matters.'[51]

A 'sense of a foreshortened future' is regarded as one key symptom of post-traumatic stress disorder (PTSD). Whether we focus on the diagnostic category of PTSD, or on a broader category of the biographical and emotional impacts of repeated trauma,[52] what can be learned from the trauma-informed literature about the impact of trauma on future orientation?

Matthew Ratcliffe and colleagues[53] emphasise the interpersonal aspects of the links between trauma, future orientation, and planning for the future:

> Projects, cares, and concerns are sustained interpersonally. Almost all goal-directed activities implicate other people in some way ... the integrity of one's projects ... depends on the integrity of those relations. Where there is pervasive uncertainty, where others cease to be dependable, where the world is unsafe and one's own abilities are in doubt, projects collapse. It is not just that the person lacks something that is presupposed by the possibility of *a specific project*. What is missing is something that the intelligibility of *projects in general* depends upon. One finds oneself in a world from which the possibility of meaningful, progressive, goal-directed activity is absent.[54]

For someone experiencing this erosion or loss of life structure, the sense of time may change: 'one confronts a world that is incompatible with the possibility of an open and progressive life story'.[55]

From a practice-based point of view (whether, for instance, in education, social work, health, or justice), how might such a loss of faith in people and structures of the world be addressed? Ratcliffe, following the ground-breaking work of Judith Lewis Herman (1992), emphasises first the nurturance of a localised sense of safety and trust, before any attempt to negotiate goals or discussing a narrative assuming a sense of the future. Herman herself[56] recognises the enormous challenges in achieving even such a first step, for example in the context of ongoing war or in the context of ongoing family or community violence. And, we might add, in the context of the precarity of services, the (non)existence of services and (in)stabilities and (dis)continuities and variability of safety of services.[57]

Alternative, crip, and queer temporalities/non-normative logics of time

> Queer uses of time and space develop in opposition to the institutions of family, heterosexuality, and reproduction, and queer subcultures develop as alternatives to kinship-based notions of community. In my work on subcultures, I explore the stretched out adolescences of queer culture makers and I posit an 'epistemology of youth' that disrupts conventional accounts of subculture, youth culture, adulthood, race, class, and maturity. ... Queer subcultures produce alternative temporalities, I will argue, by allowing their participants to believe that their futures can be imagined according to logics that lie outside of the conventional forward-moving narratives of birth, marriage, reproduction, and death.
>
> J. Halberstam, 'What's that smell? Queer temporalities and subcultural lives', 2003

I want to pick up the notion that futures may be imagined according to logics that lie outside of the conventional forward-moving narratives, as a way into the possibility of a way of thinking about *alternative temporalities* for some care-leavers.

Following Halberstam,[58] if we think of our conventional ways of considering time, especially future time, as privileged or bourgeois, as contingent on a received or pre-ordained *logic* of reproduction, family time, inheritance of values via a relatively stable family arrangement, and stable culture, it is only a small step to realise that the logics and counterlogics of some young people in transition from care will be understandably based, instead, on lengthy and repeated experience of *entirely different contingencies and temporal rhythms*: for instance, the contingencies of maltreatment, family breakdown, removal from home, the demeaning of one's own culture and language, perhaps an uncertain future of so-called care, or a tilted or skewed or biased 'playing field' of access to post-school education, work, and accommodation. And for some young people, much worse, with aspects of experience that deny any sense of human rights.[59]

Halberstam discusses the stretched out adolescences of some queer subcultures, but for young people in transition from care there may be a constriction or compression of adolescence and of emerging adulthood.[60]

In a health context, Sara Wasson[61] talks about the 'transgressive temporalities' of transplant care in which the body and mind have to *wait*, exhaustingly, for a transplant which may never arrive, with implied doubts about 'curative futurity'. For Wasson: 'In all these ways, such waiting connects with crip and queer efforts to recognise the validity of unexpected, sideways, rogue ways of approaching time beyond [a] linear progress arc.'

Emily Datskou,[62] in a paper on queer temporalities in *Wuthering Heights*, the ground-breaking nineteenth-century English novel by Emily Brontë, not only finds condensation of time and nonlinear temporalities in the novel's plot, but also in what we know about Emily Brontë's own life, which was characterised by repeated family losses.

Logic

Here in this section I want to argue that *individual* young people in real-life transition from care, whatever their approach to future-oriented planning – including, and this is key, those young people who positively *do* wish to forward plan[63] – will usually have, and show or express, a personal or autobiographical *logic*, linking aspects of planning agency – linking *what matters and who matters* – to *shared deliberations and shared planning*, and to *a sense of personal time* (see Chapters 3–7 of this book).

(Researchers and practitioners will also deploy logics about planning, but I want to focus here on young people's logics.)

This dynamic logic – which may or may not include a *counterlogic* to normative assumptions about future-oriented planning – may be regarded as forming a potential basis for practice-based collaborative and co-production work on planning (whether, for instance, in education, or social care, or health care, or justice; see Chapter 10). There are many examples of individual logics – and counterlogics – in Chapters 3–6. Nailah's account[64] of a sense of personal time – her own logic – is particularly complex (in itself, and in its relation to other aspects of planning in her lifeworld), but highly instructive for the wide range of what we might imagine for the logics of other care-experienced young people. Logics, on this account, are not overviews (by either the young person or the practitioner/researcher), or summaries, or meta-level narratives, but rather are provisional, dynamically interwoven, complex, multi-coloured tapestries. Crucially, they are dynamically embedded in (not only grounded in) real-life 'lived' experience, or, in Wittgenstein's terms, forms of life.[65]

The idea of an individual or personal logic – and our application of it to the specific contexts of planning under conditions of compounded adversity – is based on work by the philosopher Juliet Floyd (2016), writing about Wittgenstein's notions of forms of life: *Lebensform*.

I want to pick up five aspects of Floyd's account of logic: (1) logic as something fluid, dynamic, open-ended, and a matter of ongoing discussion; (2) logic as embedded in the whirl of life, with a backdrop of real-world contingencies – life structuring in life; (3) logic in relation to a comparison Floyd and Wittgenstein make between logical features of what we say or express, and facial (physiognomic) features (this raises the question, how do we get to know and recognise and *appreciate* a particular person's individual logic of planning?); (4) logic as expressive voice – the speaking of language as part of logical forms of activity, and the *suppression* of human voice; and finally (5) logic as *not* synoptic (wide-field), not meta-, *not an overview*.

Logic as something fluid

Floyd describes logic as simple, using 'ordinary ways of talking',[66] and as 'something fluid … necessarily and absolutely fluid … necessarily and absolutely a matter of ongoing discussion'.[67] Each step we take in the logical connections we actively make may be unwound, critically reflected on, contested, discussed, amalgamated, dropped, and picked up again. The *starting point* for a personal logic (about what matters, shared deliberation, cross-temporal planning, and their links) may be erased and revised. The critical reflection on a particular connection we make (for example, between a remembered experience of a parent maltreating one – and maltreating one's birth siblings – and a current discovery that the parent was herself/ himself maltreated while a child, as in Nailah's case in Chapter 5) may be re-iterated and discussed many times, and may link in a complexly logical way to our contemporary actions with those birth parents and siblings). Joe (in Chapter 6) fluidly and humorously considers whether education or friends are more important to him.

Fluid logic is provisional and sometimes quite clearly conflicted, confused, confounded – work in progress. In Charles Taylor's words: articulations are 'not simply descriptions ... on the contrary, articulations are attempts to formulate what is initially inchoate, or confused, or badly formulated'.[68] This active aspect of working logic is integral to the narratives in several of the case-based chapters, including reflexive shared discussions – about apparent 'contradictions' – between a participant and the research interviewer.

Floyd pushes the notion of fluidity to the full bounds or limits of aspect realism.[69] As discussed earlier in this book, Floyd characterises a philosophical approach which she calls aspect realism: 'without grounded metaphysics and no particular epistemology or theory of mind'.[70] For Floyd, 'aspects are modal, attaching to possibilities and necessities: fields of significance, opportunities for projecting and instantiating our concepts'.[71] She advocates very careful attention to the 'rough ground' of ordinary day-to-day language: aspect perception not as a psychological phenomenon, but as part of forms of life, as a way of structuring possible lives, based on real-life experience and real social worlds.

Floyd emphasises that logic rests on no special 'formal' features, no 'glue' (compare the relative glueiness of Bratmanian normative conceptions of cross-temporal planning with, for instance, Elijah Millgram's and Jennifer Morton's more ecologically – or contextually – aware approach to rationality norms), and no 'prior ordering' (think queer time as a counterlogic to normative or prior conceptions of time). Instead, it is our human *activities* – 'fashioning links in our world, one by one',[72] and 'plumbing the limits of certain kinds of procedures'[73] (think of the 'self-reliance' logics of Charelle or Danny in Chapter 4, and Nailah in Chapter 5[74]).

Logic as life structuring in life

We *embed* logic in life. Not only language-games,[75] but the reflexive *use* of language in the real-life whirl of human life, with its vicissitudes,[76] situated, day to day, week to week, and perhaps for whatever future there is reason to imagine.[77]

Loss of a loved one (or loss of a home) may bring with it extraordinary changes in our background cares, commitments, day-to-day lives. A logic of grief[78] might include denial while also scaffolding, making sense, and mourning. For care-leavers, losses may have been multiple and compounded, so a personal logic may, of course, be an *extraordinary work in progress* during emerging adulthood – in the superadded contexts of precarity of access to education, work, housing, and in the contexts of, for some young people, day-to-day self-management of mental health struggles (see Chapters 1 and 9, and see Chapter 4 for an example of Brittany's logic for planning in relation to her mental health issues), and/or incarceration.[79]

For Juliet Floyd, logic is both active *and* passive. The binary of 'active or passive agency?' unfolds or unravels, as a personal logic *allows some of real-life's contingencies to play out*, while we also grasp and try to comprehend what is important and what and who matters (including someone we have lost through death or 'estrangement': note Charelle's concern for her birth mother struggling in another part of the country). To use Floyd's metaphor: 'In water we may sink if we do not swim, remaining active and passive in the right ways'.[80]

This is close to Margaret Archer's wish to see reflexivity as concretely engaged with specific real-world situations, but is manifestly different from Archer's[81] perhaps too-binary account of active versus passive agency.

Logic as face – wearing a look – a dense field of significance

Juliet Floyd suggests a comparison between the living logical features of what we say (the internal relations among these) and facial features – all the aspects of an individual person's face that 'hold together', and that we eventually recognise and 'know'. For Floyd, 'acquaintance ... is nothing less than the sense in which, by looking, listening, probing, discussing and responding, we become acquainted with a *particular* person, emotion, proof, perspective, look, and so on'.[82]

And, crucially, we compare different faces and different logics (as we did in the case-based chapters, Chapters 3–6; and see Chapter 2 for methodology – comparing two cases, each with comparable foci of what matters).

'We must work by looking, responding, querying, comparing, and so on – just as we do with a living human face':[83] holding onto the sense of the aliveness and spirit and expressivity of the face – the 'logic'.

Think of portrait photography or documentary film of peoples living in particular places and times – however, we are not talking about 'culture' but rather about particular individuals, albeit in specific cultural contexts. Floyd argues that Wittgenstein's use of the word *Lebensform* – form of life – broadens and deepens 'an undifferentiated notion of culture ... opening up possibilities of expression'.[84]

Compare and contrast with the *given* logics of professionals' areas of practice: psychology and psychiatry,[85] social work (for example transition or pathway planning), education (for example particular curricula), justice (for example the logic of incarceration and its link to race), or some approaches to philosophy (logic as abstract laws of thought, purged of anything specifically person-related[86]). And the philosopher's or scientific researcher's 'craving for generality' and 'contemptuous attitude towards the particular case'.[87]

For Floyd the 'I', the subject, the agent, "is embedded in the fluidity, the interactional situatedness, of voice, procedure, and expression.'[88]

Logic as expressive voice, and making sense of the suppression of voice

Let's consider speaking, or indeed performing, as part of logical compositional and improvisational activity, and as part of a form of life. For Floyd (and Wittgenstein) 'the basic context is a social one'.[89]

In interviews, for example, chains of remarks, narratives, drawn or painted pictures, or chosen or taken photographs, diagrams, are *offered* and *shown* to, for example, a researcher or practitioner. A 'whole world of internal (logical) relations'[90] (think face) may come to life, both for the person expressing these linked-up thoughts and feelings, and for a listener who is free to actively listen and make sense, or, by consent, share the making sense.

Values show forth, are expressed, in that we follow them, argue over them, surrender them, and so on.

A chain of articulated expression 'draws out *aspects* of thoughts, given in fields of necessity, contingency, and possibility'.[91] Compare the *composition* of songs and music, and their orchestration/interpretation, or the playing of a game in which the parameters change continuously. One young person in our research, in transition from care, discussed his own patterns of internal conversations and

> outlined in considerable detail his 'process of thought' which was complex and flexible. He discussed it reflexively: its origins and its current usages, and the metaphors and models it was based on, including football. The positions of different members of a football team acted as a metaphor for thinking differently and responsively as situations change and 'they have to rethink their process of thought'.[92]

As in later Wittgenstein, '*how* we link, what we specifically do *in* linking, become[s] a thoroughgoing, integrated part of logic, part of life itself'.[93]

When we consider the suppression of voice, this may be mundane or 'ordinary'. Floyd points out that philosophers, including Plato, 'worried about the suppression of human voice in the face of writing'[94] (that is, writing systems, alphabets, graphic codes, and literacy).[95]

But the suppression of voice may not be mundane: one care-leaving participant says, after reflecting on recalled childhood abuse: "How do I express myself again?" And the same participant, after currently attempting to communicate certain important matters to a public service, said: "I'm being put down for coming and speaking my, expressing myself, so yeah."

Logic as not synoptic (wide-field), and not an overview, not a master narrative

For Floyd, a chain of logic has no direction or orientation – forward or backward are 'ultimately metaphorical'.[96] (Compare with our discussion earlier on alternative temporalities; compare with dreams; compare with aspects of play; and a sense of personal time.) This in contrast to a pointing finger which may accurately indicate what I am looking at, or where I am going, or what you would like me to look at, or where you are headed – what or where your goal might be.

Instead, Floyd emphasises the 'profusion of interwovenness'[97] and 'orchestration'[98] of logic, the journeying and composition and improvisation of further articulation, further communication, iteration, returning, rearranging, and never an overview or summary.

For Floyd, following Wittgenstein, understanding and actively using logic requires: 'the metaphor of the city as an evolving organized whole, its "downtown" heart centered on winding, ancient parts rather than straight-running superhighways.'[99]

9

Emotions: a background framework is called into question

If we go back to Chapters 3–6 it is clear that the young people we interviewed expressed emotions, sometimes very strongly felt emotions. When participants articulated what and who matters, this was done with feeling. When forward planning was discussed, some participants rejected the idea of planning ahead with feeling. Moreover, the research interview's focus on internal conversations often triggered participant-led discussions about very strong, often profound, accounts of emotions linked to birth parents and siblings, foster parents and foster siblings, peers and friends, and sometimes services and professionals. To take one example, anger[1] was expressed by Charelle in the context of discussing one priority for 'what matters' – her housing accommodation – and her deep sense that no-one is looking after her:

> 'Well if I don't have a roof over my head, I can't do anything. That is obviously my main thing 'cos I ain't got no mum, no guardian, or anyone to look after me so if I ain't looking after me, who is? No-one else ain't feeding me, no-one else ain't bathing me, so it's me, I come first.'

Alongside deeply felt and deeply thoughtful accounts of what and who matters we hear extended and poignant narratives about distressing aspects of inner lives. For Nailah and Tyreece there is a sense that their troubled inner lives are sometimes emotionally *overwhelming*. Nailah feels that "bullying made permanent damage to me and how I view myself". For Tyreece, at the end of the second interview, he says: "when I consider my problems, I just get overwhelmed by emotion." Tyreece is so angry with his estranged father that he cannot discuss him, except by using an expletive, and then the briefest of discussion in his otherwise deeply thoughtful interviews. Nailah "still hates" her "past" but discusses how she is beginning to understand how her parents came to abuse and neglect her, and how she copes by reframing her expectations of her relationships with them – "treat them as a friend".

Tyreece connects what he calls his overthinking – "my brain just shoots things at me" – to his family "taking the piss so much" about his physical appearance when he was a child. He reflects: "they didn't think at the time it was affecting me but look what it did to me now ... I used to overthink and that's when it all started." And now, "I look in the mirror and I'm not really like a fine person in myself ... when you have confidence in yourself then you're good, but that's the one thing I don't have." Carefully, he goes on to say: "I only gather that when I have people around me that I know believe in me and trust in me."

There are three sections to this chapter.

The first section is concerned with philosopher Martha Nussbaum's 'upheavals of thought'.[2] Nussbaum, in her influential book on the intelligence of emotions, *Upheavals of Thought* (2001), quotes Marcel Proust[3] on love producing 'real geological upheavals of thought', ' a mountain range had abruptly thrust itself into view, hard as rock', 'Rage, Jealousy, Curiosity, Envy, Hate, Suffering, Pride, Astonishment, and Love'. For Nussbaum, emotions 'mark our lives as uneven, uncertain, and prone to reversal'.[4] For young people in transition from care the words 'prone to reversal', 'uneven', and 'uncertain' might bring a wry smile.

The second section considers philosopher Matthew Ratcliffe's approach to emotions and emotional intentionality. His work, especially his work on loss and grief,[5] may provide a philosophical building block for thinking about the impact of the repeated 'upheavals' and rifts of life and lifeworlds experienced by young people in care. His work helps to extend our sense of what planning and intentionality might look like, and what sense young people make of this under conditions of repeated emotional rupture. Ratcliffe discusses the notion of a 'wider-ranging disturbance of the experiential world within which the object of emotion is experienced'.[6] For young people in care, of course, a 'background framework' to a lifeworld is called into question repeatedly/recurrently.

In the third section, I reflect on some of the implications of these ideas to care-leavers' planning during the transition from care, focusing on multiple emotion ruptures, the importance of understanding emotion-based aspects of development (including, in particular, the opportunities of emerging adulthood), transition itself as a potential – and complex – emotion rupture, and particular emotion-based aspects of transition (including mental health issues). I prepare the ground for discussion of anger and other complex emotions in Chapter 10, on 'voice'.

Martha Nussbaum on 'upheavals of thought'

In her book entitled *Upheavals of Thought: The Intelligence of the Emotions*, Martha Nussbaum portrays emotions as 'intelligent responses to the perception of value'.[7] In Chapter 1, she discusses her own experience, as an adult, of the loss of her mother. She says:

> In the weeks that followed, I had periods of agonized weeping; whole days of crushing fatigue; nightmares in which I felt altogether unprotected and alone, and seemed to feel a strange animal walking across my bed. I felt, again, anger – at the nurses for not prolonging her life until I arrived … it seemed appropriate to be angry … above all I felt anger at myself.[8]

Nussbaum identifies several aspects of emotions as fundamental: 'First of all, they [emotions] are *about* something: they have an object' [9] For Nussbaum, her complex emotions were about her mother. In the contexts of leaving care, a young person's complex emotions might be about a birth parent or foster parent, or birth siblings, or indeed about the recent loss of a family member during transition. The object may also be an event or process such as the memory of a move from one placement to another, or a troubling housing accommodation transition, or the transition process.

Nussbaum continues: 'Second, the object is an *intentional* object: that is, it figures in the emotion as it is seen or interpreted by the person whose emotion it is.'[10] For Nussbaum, an emotion is not simply or passively experienced, it is focused and directed; and it is 'internal, and embodies a way of seeing'. Tyreece's anger at his father was connected to a range of autobiographical experience, most of which was unspoken; Nailah's anger at her parents was able to be spoken about: both participants experienced emotions and 'a way of seeing'.

And further: 'Third, these emotions embody not simply ways of seeing an object, but beliefs – often very complex – about the object.'[11] Nussbaum provides the example of anger, in which a complex and detailed set of beliefs may be at play, that is, that some damage has occurred to 'me or to something or someone close to me'. In Virginia Eatough et al's 2008 study of women's anger:

> Perceptions of injustice and unfair treatment figured large in the participants' accounts of their anger. They described events from their childhood with the same sort of feeling they showed for more recent situations. Moreover, they felt anger when they perceived injustice toward others as well as themselves. Their perceptions give rise to intense emotions.[12]

For Nussbaum there is a fourth aspect to emotions: 'Finally [emotions are] concerned with *value*', their object as invested with value or importance 'for some role it plays in the person's own life'.[13] The value makes reference to the person's own flourishing, and 'they take their stand in my own life',[14] and 'have to do with whatever I do value, however well or badly those things fit together'.[15] Brittany[16] loves being with, and spends planned time with, her foster parents' own children, giving us a sense of what she values and the potential role these children play, and have played, in her own life. Although Brittany does not feel able to think too much about the future, she is clear about what and who matter, and how that is connected to her own sense of herself and her own flourishing.

But what more can we learn about Nussbaum's point about 'however well or badly those things fit together'. What if a young person has a history of repeated losses and ruptures as described in Chapter 1? Where does that leave the young person during her emerging adulthood, during her transition from care?

Matthew Ratcliffe: emotional intentionality

The philosopher Matthew Ratcliffe is among a number of scholars who have suggested that emotions have a very particular form of intentionality.[17] I outline six aspects of Ratcliffe's complex view. At the same time I interweave aspects of philosopher Rupert Read's (2018)[18] account of grief, in which he asks the question: Can there be a logic of grief?

Emotion as rupture in a person's lifeworld

Ratcliffe acknowledges that his view of the emotions speaks in particular to those emotions such as grief in which a 'rupture' has taken place in a person's experience, calling into question the existing 'world' or lifeworld. Ratcliffe quotes Martha Nussbaum's words on hearing about the death of her mother: 'violently tears the fabric of hope, planning, and expectation that I have built up around her all my life.'[19] The event calls into question the world as we know it, including our 'background framework' of practices, cares, concerns, commitments, and life's possibilities, or future possibilities.

Rupert Read, like Nussbaum, writes from personal experience – in his case the loss of 'a very close friend ... utterly unexpectedly – "prematurely"'.[20] He describes grief as a 'deformation of one's lifeworld', 'metaphorically ... having a hole punched into (or ripped out of) one's lived world'. Grief, for Read, involves an 'actual loss of an integral part of one's very world'.[21]

For young people in transition from care there may have been *repeated* ruptures in their lifeworlds, repeated experiences of a world undermined (see Chapter 1): and these during their formative/developmental years, while they are learning about – and contributing to – how worlds of emotions and social relationships feel 'for me'.

A background framework is called into question

On Ratcliffe's account, the rupture occurs: 'against a backdrop of interconnected, habitual activities and patterns of thought. These depend for their intelligibility on variably integrated cares, commitments, and concerns'.[22]

For a child or adolescent the background framework is her day-to-day family and social life, including school life, however problematic each of these may be. For young people coming into care, ruptures occur (and, in the contexts of maltreatment, and/or polyvictimisation, *will* have occurred) across multiple life contexts.[23]

The 'background framework' is also in some sense deeply layered, layered and interwoven so much so that the full implications – of a loss, or losses – cannot possibly be understood or 'spelt out' immediately; rather there may be a felt sense that 'something will have profound repercussions'.[24]

The full implications are impossible to 'pin down'

For Ratcliffe, in the case of grief, there is a particular form of uncertainty, incomprehension, and 'recognition that something is lost from the world as a whole'; that 'certain things no longer make sense'.[25] The sense that this is 'unfathomable' translates into a language, not only of uncertainty, but of reflexive questioning about 'everything'. Ratcliffe is clear that 'It is not simply that [the person] has trouble updating a holistic network of propositional beliefs'.[26]

Life may seem surreal, unreal. Our language reaches out for metaphors of undermining or earthquakes – metaphors that draw attention to the sense of no longer knowing what one's bedrock is – of thinking, and feeling.

In the narratives from young people in Chapters 3–6, the emotion of anger, or even rage, seemed to link to a sense of incomprehension: fury at loss, and rage at the breaking of multiple boundaries and repeated violations of reasonable expectations of parents and professionals.

The two-sidedness of emotional intentionality

The aspects of emotional intentionality discussed so far have been concerned with the rupture or ruptures in a person's lifeworld *and* in a 'background framework' of cares and commitments – profound real-world/lifeworld disruptions which cannot necessarily be put into words.

Indeed a central claim of Ratcliffe's approach is that 'emotional intentionality has a distinctive "two-sided" structure'.[27] There is the 'object' of the emotion (what the emotion is 'about', for example the loss of a loved one or the anticipation of a major personally disruptive event[28]) and there is the 'potential or actual disturbance of the experienced world *within* which the object of one's emotion is encountered'.[29] He contrasts our usual 'pre-made' world in which we can reasonably assume that it is possible to make decisions and 'go on' normally, with the emotionally ruptured world he characterises in which *both* the object of the emotion is 'in transition', or is no longer present, and the background framework within which we see the world is also called profoundly into question – the object *and* the background context are 'geologically' destabilised.

If I experience the beginnings of an earthquake (real or metaphorical), then it isn't only the 'geological' happening of the 'actual' earthquake that is important, it is also my living space, my day-to-day life, the existences of my loved ones, and my own survival that are called into question.

Again, for young people in transition from care, the two-sidedness, of loss *and* loss of 'background framework' may have happened repeatedly, or should we say 'compoundedly', in that each rupture may seem to be 'connected' to the previous one (for example repeated moves of placement) but in ways that may seem to make little sense to the young person,[30] and without the (planning) agency of the young person?

A way of revising the world

In a crucial step, Ratcliffe, noting again the work of Martha Nussbaum, includes within his model the idea of emotions as intelligent – emotional intentionality as a form of recognition, and 'of engaging with and making sense of one's situation'.[31] He sees the shape and form of emotional intentionality as making revision of the world possible. It constitutes a 'broader rationality'.

Rupert Read[32] suggests that the frequently described 'denial' that often occurs as part of grief is not helpfully seen as the opposite of acceptance, but rather as a logical part of – or transitional towards – acceptance. Denial as not absurd, not irrational, but an understandable and 'profound difficulty of marrying one's beliefs with the facts *even as one assents to them*'.[33] The 'fluidity' of Juliet

Floyd's characterisation of logic comes to mind (see previous chapter). The expression of the paradox is perhaps constitutive of progress – progress that is likely to take time.

A broader rationality (and revision) takes time

If our personal worlds are 'upended' by emotional ruptures, then the process of revision will inevitably take time. Ratcliffe makes this aspect of emotional intentionality – a temporal process – crucial to his model. Emotional ruptures are not episodic, not brief, cannot be 'navigated swiftly',[34] and cannot be 'rationally' described. Their imports and implications are wide-ranging and destabilising. They impact loves, long-term commitments, cares, concerns – they impact what matters and who matters.

Revision will take time, but critically, *active revision* is part of the distinctive 'work' of the broader rationality/intentionality of the emotions, as characterised by Ratcliffe.

Is it helpful to see scepticism or rejection of future-oriented planning as part of 'active revision' – in the light of repeated emotion ruptures – for some young people; an alternative temporality with specific meanings, a specific logic that makes personal sense – a sense of personal time (see previous chapter)?

(The process of active revision may not be 'easy to see' for friends, family, professionals, researchers, especially in the context of historic repeated ruptures, *and* the current demands of finding accommodation, finding work, staying in education, and so on.)

Also discussing time and gradual revision, Rupert Read argues that:

> the logic of grief is the logic of being a person, part of a whole of persons [one's significant others] that is prior to its parts. And the logic of being (and becoming) necessarily in time ... the kind of being that sometimes non-irrationally grieves ... in the impossible but nevertheless actual loss of an integral part of one's very world.[35]

Read also suggests that the temporal and the personal are a vital dimension of the logical. Variations in how a personal logic (in

Read's example in relation to grief, but more generally in relation to emotion ruptures) plays out will vary from person to person and from context to context.[36]

Logic in the broadest sense (see Chapter 8) and not in the sense of laws of thought 'in some pure abstract sense, purged of anything specifcally persons-related'.[37]

Transition from out-of-home care

In thinking about the work of these theorists, and bearing closely in mind the emotion-infused narratives of the young people we interviewed (see Chapters 3–7), there are several points to consider.

Multiple emotion ruptures

Care-leavers are likely to have experienced multiple emotion ruptures, happening over time. Each may 'call into question the background world'[38] – Ratcliffe's two-sided structure of emotional intentionality. The young person may wonder: what *does* matter? Who *does* matter?

Indeed, how extraordinary – of course our human reflexivity *is* extraordinary[39] – that participants (see Chapters 3–6) did have such articulate answers to the question about what matters, even if some had decided that forward planning was problematic. Equally, no wonder that some young people feel that 'permanent damage has been done' or that 'there is something wrong with me'.

Development during emerging adulthood[40]

These lifeworld ruptures or perturbations or deformations occur during the formative developmental years of childhood and adolescence, but with the opportunity during late adolescence and emerging adulthood – the focus of this book – to make sense of, review, revise, reframe, rethink, form new and renewed relationships, and plan – in the broadest and most flexible sense (compare our accounts of logic in the previous chapter, following Floyd and Read in this chapter).

Transition itself as a rupture

The long-drawn-out process of transition from care, with its potential losses and micro-losses of support, will likely be an object itself of emotion (Nussbaum) and emotional intentionality (Ratcliffe's and Read's characterisations of emotional rupture, requiring ongoing revision), and potential psychological difficulties.[41] As one example, recall Nailah (Chapter 5) and the logic of her sense of time before and during transition, and her complex sense of the future.

Particular aspects of experiences before and during transition

Nussbaum's and Ratcliffe's characterisation of emotion as a 'way of revising the world' and the 'intelligence of the emotions' may help us begin to understand some very particular phenomenological[42] and hermeneutic[43] aspects of care-leavers' experience: survivalist self-reliance;[44] forward planning scepticism (see Chapter 3–7); and crucially, the high prevalence of mental health issues.[45]

Emotion-informed (and trauma-informed) approaches to planning would emphasise both an awareness of the impact of repeated ruptures on a young person's planning and an awareness of the potential for revision and reconstitution over time.[46]

Planning and voice: starting points

By voice I mean voice. Listen, I will say, thinking that in one sense the answer is simple. And then I will remember how it felt to speak when there was no resonance, how it was when I began writing, how it still is for many people, how it still is for me sometimes. To have a voice is to be human. To have something to say is to be a person. But speaking depends on listening and being heard: it is an intensely relational act.

Carol Gilligan, *In a Different Voice*, 1993, p xvi

Introduction

Carol Gilligan's work has helped bring a re-imagined range of ways of seeing, ways of hearing the voices of, and ways of talking about young people – young women, but also young people who are different in so many different ways. Gilligan's *Letter to Readers*, written in 1993 as a new Preface to her original and groundbreaking 1982 book *In a Different Voice: Psychological Theory and Women's* Development,[1] brings 19 pages of insight upon insight, and I encourage readers – 'if there's one thing you read today' – to read or re-read Gilligan's 19 pages, and of course also her book.

As readers will be aware, our book is concerned with beginning to think about planning differently, more broadly, and more flexibly, with a clear focus on young adults experiencing compounded adversity.

The journey of the book began with young people's own voices – a seemingly strong rejection, by some care-leavers, of future-oriented planning, and in parallel, an expressive and clear focus on what is important: what matters and who matters. Furthermore, a commitment by some young people to shared deliberations with friends, family, and (sometimes) professionals.

Expressive emotion infused each of these aspects of planning. And expressive emotion had shape and direction.

In this final chapter I want to return to these starting points: young people's own voices, their own expressive starting points, their rich hoards of experience, their own senses of what is important, their own (autobiographical) logics and counterlogics, their own multiple forms of reflexivities, their own contradictions, their own strength of feeling – including anger – about their worlds; their own 'takes' on shared deliberation, shared agency, and the vital importance of friends and/or family; and their own individual approaches to time and planning.

In this chapter I ask the question: can young people's *own starting points* for planning also be the starting points of services, or potential services,[2] starting points for research and service co-design and co-production, and starting points for individual help and support? Each of these areas is by definition *planful* in some sense: but whose sense?

I said I would attempt to indicate the implications for practice of the research reported in this book. While writing the book, beginning to read some of the literature on co-design[3] and co-production, as an opportunity for the expression of and recognition of young people's voices, has had a strong effect on how I have envisaged this last chapter. The across-sector co-design literatures (to be discussed later) have made me completely re-think the implications of the research we conducted in (little) England.

So, this chapter, in addressing the question about young people's own starting points – implicating both voice *and* 'listening and being heard' – has four primary sections. I begin with the poet and playwright Lemn Sissay's inspirational phrase 'flags in the mountainside'. Second, I discuss recognition theory, a major source of contemporary thought – and debate – about voice, and the struggle for minoritised peoples to be heard. Third, I discuss participatory co-design, an approach to research and practice which provides an opportunity for young people's voices not only to be heard, but also to be included in actively defining the scope and form of a project.[4] In this section I discuss a wider literature on co-design and co-production, arguing that there is much to be gained from a cross-fertilisation of ideas. Fourth, as an example of cross-fertilisation across the wider expanses of the literature on co-design – in relation to the research reported in this book – I tentatively apply the notion of 'methodological sensitivities for co-producing knowledge through enduring trustful partnerships'[5] to co-design of transition planning with young people in transition from out-of-home care.

Flags in the mountainside

> I grew my dreadlocks in Wood End. I twist my Afro hair each night at Wood End. I write every day in recreation hour. I have written poems ever since I came into care. They become my flags in the mountainside. They chart the journey.
>
> Lemn Sissay, *My Name Is Why: A Memoir*, 2019, p173

Lemn Sissay[6] is a British-Ethiopian poet and playwright who has written about his removal from his mother's care and his life in foster care and institutional care in England in the late part of the twentieth century.[7]

Lemn Sissay's phrase: 'flags in the mountainside'[8] has kept returning to me as I have been writing this book. For Sissay, flags were poems he wrote, and 'they chart[ed] the journey'. But flags were also his hair: 'There is a freedom. My hair rises into a knotted mass of twisted spikes and then the locks drop into a crown of dreadlocks.'[9]

After a series of 'placements' Sissay had been found himself, age 17, in an 'assessment centre', but with the help of Margaret Parr of the National Association of Young People in Care (NAYPIC), he was eventually allowed to attend the Black and In Care conference on 20 October 1984',[10] and out of that conference came a Black and In Care video that was watched by many social services departments around the country. Upon returning to his assessment centre (Wood End) after the conference, Sissay notes: 'Exhilarated, I returned to Wood End where I was strip-searched.'[11]

We discuss respect and disrespect, and we discuss anger, in the contexts of 'care' later. But perhaps we can borrow 'flags in the mountainside' as a metaphor for young people's own starting points, their emotionally expressive accounts of what matters and who matters, their shared deliberations and shared actions, their accounts of their own sense of time and planning?

Recognition theory has much to say about peoples' struggles to gain respect and overcome disrespect.

Recognition theory: recognition, respect, and disrespect

In historian Peter E. Gordon's words[12] reviewing philosopher Axel Honneth's recent work:

> All of us need recognition. We need it from those we love but also from the state if we are to enjoy our rights as citizens, and from society at large if we are to secure esteem for our achievements. In the absence of recognition we languish, unloved and unseen, without legal protection and without the basic sense that we matter as human beings.

Or, in Axel Honneth's own recent words:

> The concept of 'recognition' ... has become a crucial element of our political and cultural self-understanding, as is illustrated by demands that we respect each other as equally entitled members of a cooperative community, that we unconditionally recognise the particularity of others or respect cultural minorities in the context of the 'politics of recognition'.[13]

Honneth talks about the *struggle* for recognition. He sees societies developing via individual struggles and collective resistance, 'in which a shared language is found for feelings of having been unjustly treated, a language that points – however indirectly – to possibilities for expanding relationships of recognition'.[14]

He leaves open the question of an end-point for social change – as he says: 'this is no longer a matter for theory but rather for the future of social struggles'.[15]

Disrespect and the denial of recognition are regarded as unjust 'not simply because it harms subjects or restricts their freedom to act, but because it injures them with regard to the positive understanding of themselves that they have acquired intersubjectively'.[16] Honneth discusses physical maltreatment, or 'violation of the body' as 'a type of disrespect that affects a person at the level of physical integrity'.[17] He further develops the notion of disrespect to include denigration, social ostracism, and social-structural exclusion from legitimate rights, leading to potential loss of self-respect – 'a loss of the ability to relate to oneself as a legally equal interaction partner with all fellow humans'.[18] In addition, Honneth describes a 'third type of degradation' – 'the denigration of individual or collective ways of life', leading potentially to the position of not being able to relate to one's own mode of life as something of positive significance within one's own community.[19] He discusses shame, in each of these circumstances, as being a 'motivational impetus for a struggle for recognition'.[20]

Charles Taylor, also writing about recognition in the 1990s,[21] talks about the importance of respect and recognition both 'on an intimate plane' and in the public sphere. He notes that both domains of recognition involve dialogue and struggle, and notes that feminist scholarship has worked to understand the links and interplay between the two levels.[22] On the question of the public sphere he discusses the continuing politics of equal recognition, a point developed a quarter of a century later by Amy Gutmann, in a discussion of Taylor's original lecture/essay):

> To appreciate Taylor's prescience, we need only examine the news today in the United States, where the relationship of group recognition to individual identity is made manifest in issues ranging from the Black Lives Matter movement to the choice and use of pronouns to respect gender and sexual orientation.[23]

Honneth's and Taylor's ground-breaking work has led to a rich literature of ongoing discussion, and a recent major publication by Honneth (2021) on the modern history (in Europe) of the idea of recognition.[24] There has also been rich and (appropriately) dialogue-based dispute and discussion.[25] Here I summarise one area of critique.[26]

There is concern at the apparent failure of recognition theory to grasp the role of power in the settler-colonial relationship. Recognition 'conferred', given, or bestowed by the state may be, in effect, meaningless, with sought consent (for instance about land) as a 'ruse',[27] and states' recognition as freedom-diminishing, rather than freedom-enhancing. The grave injustices and 'perverse logics' of coloniality suggest limits to the idea of recognition in postcolonial contexts.[28] This is directly relevant to young people in transition from care: children from Indigenous families are overrepresented in care and leaving care populations in several countries.[29] And the mental health of Indigenous populations is known to be compromised and impacted by a 'shattering legacy of European colonization … [with] brutal histories of land possession, military conquest, forced settlement, religious repression, and coercive assimilation'.[30]

Peter Gordon's characterisation of the broad basis for recognition theory, our need for recognition from those we love, from the state, from society, and his reminding us that without recognition we 'languish, unloved and unseen, without legal protection and without the basic sense that we matter as human beings',[31] summarises the importance of this theoretical area. But how might we build on this, together with the critiques of recognition theory, to consider the implications of the work reported in this book for transition planning? One answer is to regard co-design, with its potential for multi-level recognition, as a key contemporary foundation for re-imagining the future of cross-disciplinary services and support for young people in transition from out-of-home care.

Co-design

Being playfully quantitative, the perspective of this book on planning during the transition from out-of-home care shifts the 'score' for some young people from 'minus 1' (apparent 'lack' of future orientation, suggesting the need perhaps for an 'intervention') to '+3' (at least three reflexive areas of planning agency which a young person 'has', and may choose – actively and expressively – to bring to co-design and co-production).

There is a fascinating literature within the transition from out-of-home care field on co-design, co-production, and other forms of participatory and peer research and service development.[32] But before addressing this specific literature, I want to use a larger frame to attempt to make fertile connections across fields.

In a recent global review of modes of co-production for sustainability,[33] including 32 initiatives from six continents, focusing on reshaping how ecosystems can be managed for sustainability, six modes of co-production were evident: researching solutions; empowering voices; brokering power; reframing power; navigating differences (across power differentials); and reframing agency (creating safe spaces to identify collective forms of agency capable of addressing systemic governance issues).[34] The authors 'encourage the application of our heuristic as a reflexive tool to open dialogue and strengthen transparency in design choices in co-production processes [for sustainability]'.[35] It is of interest that each of the modes identified by these authors echoes aspects of co-design and co-production in other fields, or overlapping fields, such as active decolonial climate change work, young people's mental health care, transition from out-of-home care, and co-production approaches that integratively address trauma (including cross-generational and postcolonial effects of trauma). Let us very briefly consider some of these overlapping areas.

In a recent paper from Aotearoa New Zealand, geographer and sustainability scientist Alison Greenaway and colleagues point out: 'The well-being of a significant share of the planet depends on the institutions and actions of Indigenous peoples who are connected to over a quarter of the world's land surface.'[36]

Yet, as these authors note, Indigenous knowledge systems remain constrained by Western methodologies and theoretical frameworks. In their paper, these authors discuss a relational framing (*manuhiri*) offered by Māori in Aotearoa New Zealand. This leads to a range of different co-governance, co-management, and co-planning arrangements, including intentional creating of spaces (in organisations, budgets, funding processes) for Indigenous knowledge and practices. During their co-research programmes:

> The analogy of the *waka taurua* (two connected boats navigating together[37]) was shared by colleagues ... a powerful signifier of the deep knowledge produced through centuries of Pacific navigating ... a gift to Western science ... and a pivotal organising symbol for Te Mana Rauhī Taioa – Environmental Protection Authority in Aotearoa New Zealand.[38]

The profound effects of climate change, particularly as it impacts on Indigenous populations, are also seen on heritage – inherited traditions, monuments, objects, places, and culture, as well as contemporary knowledge drawn from these. Heritage may be tangible or intangible, including cultural practices and a sense of place.[39] Local and indigenous knowledge, which may be regarded as a form of intangible heritage, is impacted by climate change, affecting loss of livelihoods and migration. Decolonising climate change research – in relation to heritage – would depend on epistemic freedom,[40] requiring a decentering from the agendas of the Global North.

In the context of a co-design education programme with young adults from Ntaria in the Central Desert of Australia, Nicola St John and Yoko Akama[41] describe their work of 'catalysing a change of pace', and waiting, of setting aside research schedules and timing, of beginning to appreciate the 'complex legacies of discrimination, inter-generational trauma'. For one of the authors 'it was personally challenging and emotional in ways I didn't expect'. A 'slower rhythm of engagement' allowed 'listening to and learning from the young adults, their perspectives, and their world'.[42] As the authors acknowledge, premising 'waiting' as a form of collaboration is challenging for practitioners and researchers with their time-scheduled budgets, grants, and lives. But, these authors point out, 'waiting' is not about a 'stage' of preparation for collaborative and partnership work, but about being responsive to others (and what matters to others) in their place and time.

As mentioned earlier, there is a significant international literature on service and research co-design, co-creation, and co-production, peer research, and participation by young people in transition from out-of-home care.[43] In one recent and wide-ranging practice-based review, Jo Dixon and colleagues discuss participation, consultation, peer research, and co-production: 'arguably [the] most contemporary approach ... in both research and development', and a range of other opportunities for young people leaving care to participate in decision-making and design of services. Summarising, the authors note the importance of young people having a voice, but add: 'it is important that we also listen to and act upon what is being voiced about the research we are conducting or the services we are delivering'.[44] Research on co-design in young people's mental health care is also of central importance here, bearing in mind the known prevalence of mental health issues, including post-trauma issues, among young people leaving care.[45]

Indeed, a key element of participatory research in all health and social care contexts is to consider trauma-informed aspects of the research.[46] Although the literature on this aspect of co-design and co-production is smaller than might be expected, it does intersect with other central elements of international co-design and co-production research: issues of power and equity, the question of ensuring *all* voices[47] are heard (including those who have been silenced during trauma, and again post-trauma[48]), the enduring impact of settler–colonial social processes. In the specific example of young people in transition from out-of-home care, while trauma-informed approaches to services for children in care, and young people in transition from care, have very carefully been addressed in the literature,[49] further (participatory) thought on trauma-informed aspects of co-design and co-produced research for young people in transition from care will be important, as indeed will a range of ethical issues (for instance, reporting of ethical procedures was reported as 'inadequate' in a recent systematic review of co-design studies in health and disability for Indigenous and other children and young people [up to and including age 24] from priority social groups[50]).

In summary, I have very briefly discussed examples of co-design and co-production in sustainable development of ecosystems, the transition from out-of-home care, young people's mental health care, and co-production approaches that integratively address trauma.

These areas have potentially fruitful conceptual and material overlaps. For instance, crucially, there may be conceptual overlaps between some of the enduring changes that we may wish to make in the way our societies care for children and young people, and the enduring ways in which we may choose to make sustainable changes to the ways we care for our planet.

Such across-sector enduring changes may, almost by definition, need enduring and trustful relational partnerships during co-design and co-production.[51]

In addition, there is, in this wider literature on co-design and co-production, a clear awareness of the urgency of mutual recognition, participation, and urgency of justice in research and service development, including, crucially, a focus toward those who are most deeply affected by historic injustice, minoritisation, and state establishment of boundaries and notions of 'worthy' citizenship.[52]

In a deliberately cross-fertilising 'way forward' that is central to this final chapter, and which addresses the question asked at the beginning of the chapter (that is, can young people's *own starting points* for planning also be the starting points of services, or potential services,[53] starting points for research and service co-design and co-production, and starting points for individual help and support? Each of these areas is by definition *planful* in some sense: but whose sense?), I suggest that we might apply Alison Greenaway's (and colleagues) concept of 'methodological sensitivities for co-producing knowledge through enduring trustful partnerships'.

Methodological sensitivities for co-producing knowledge through enduring trustful partnerships

> Co-produced knowledge must include a focus on unsettling the research and management ethics and practices which fragment knowledge of nature and society and disconnect people from environments.
>
> (Greenaway et al, 2022, p 434)

In their justice-based co-working with Indigenous populations in Aotearoa New Zealand, Alison Greenaway and colleagues have sytematically co-developed a range of *relational* methodologies which recognise the enduring commitments required on all sides for this gradual work, and provide a way forward from the 'paralysis generated when non-Indigenous partners become cognisant of the enormity of devastation their Indigenous partners are working through'.[54]

Methodologies for these authors are therefore not only methodologies, but also *methodological sensitivities for co-producing knowledge through enduring trustful partnerships* – each word counting. As an example, one (of nine) co-created methodological sensitivities is 'alternative worlds are becoming visible and possible', with an impact of 'respectfully including new and marginalised actors enables framing for a plurality of worlds'.[55] The authors note that methodological sensitivities would 'need refining for each context'.[56]

Greenaway and her colleagues specify how *particular methodological sensitivities* impact on *ways of knowing and doing 'environments'*.[57] As mentioned earlier, nine are listed in their paper, co-developed for their particular caring for the environment/sustainability context.

The question arises: would this specific co-design paradigm 'transfer' to co-design with specific communities of young people in transition from out-of-home care, with whom a range of methodological sensitivities might be co-developed with an impact on *ways of knowing and feeling and doing 'planning'*?[58]

Let us look at this potential in a bit more detail, albeit sketched for preliminary collaborative discussion with care-experienced young people in specific local contexts.

Planning – a new approach

Following the case-based chapters (Chapters 3–7), and the detailed theoretical work discussed in Chapter 8, there is reason to think that instead of there being perhaps one starting point for planning – future-oriented goal-setting – there may be at least three: what matters and who matters, shared deliberation and shared planning, and a sense of personal time.

And Chapter 9 brought an emphasis on the intelligence of emotions, emotion intentionality, and the sense, following Ratcliffe's work, that a broader rationality (and revision) take time, a theme which is fundamental to the present chapter The emotional expressivity of young people's approaches to all aspects of planning has been emphasised throughout this book.

Emily R. Munro, a leading international researcher in child welfare and the transition from out-of-home care, in a recent chapter on upholding young people's rights in care and during the transition from out-of-home care, discusses the right to participation in the planning process – for young people leaving care – as a key area for reform:

> The Guidelines (General Assembly of the United Nations, 2010) acknowledge that preparation and planning are important foundations to support positive transitions from out of home care. Youth have a right to participate in decisions affecting their lives and their wishes and feelings to be given due weight. Participation has a number of benefits: it can contribute to a sense of mastery and control and build self-esteem, which are all resources that promote resilience. However, research suggests that, too often, youth participation in planning is absent, limited, or tokenistic, and youth in out of home care feel that even when they give their views these do not necessarily influence decisions concerning the timing of transition or aftercare provision.[59]

How might the new perspective on planning discussed in this book be applied to a co-design approach to transition planning?

Let us first discuss (three aspects of) planning, and second expressive language and emotion – the example of anger.

Three aspects of planning

The three-aspects approach to planning discussed in this book would be of potential relevance – and this is a key point – to both the service planning implicated in any innovative specialised aftercare/ extended care service co-design process (including, for instance, co-design of new or re-imagined forms of transition planning), *and* to an understanding and appreciation and recognition of individual young people's participation in actual day-to-day transition and aftercare preparation and planning – where that service is already available. I focus largely here on the first of these – participation in (new) service co-design for transition planning.[60]

What matters and who matters

As we saw in Chapter 8, for Bratman,[61] 'certain plan-states concern what matters in the sense of having weight in our deliberative thought'. In Chapters 3–6 we discussed examples of participants' detailed and expressive accounts of what carries weight in examples of what matters and who matters in their day-to-day lives (with implications for understanding individual young people's planning).

In an innovative service co-design process a range of detailed accounts of *what matters in transition planning* might be discussed. Clearly most transition planning is done by young people themselves in their informal social networks, as they begin to picture leaving care, and as they cope with the sudden 'cliff-edge' changes in life circumstances and in forms of support. If a transition or extended care service exists, how might that be designed via the voices/starting points of young people themselves? Some matters, during a co-design process, might not be easily or readily discussed. The area might be too personal, or difficult to put into words, the matter might be so fundamental as to defy initial attempts to understand, especially across settler-colonial divides[62] of understanding.

Alison Greenaway's emphasis on 'enduring trustful partnerships', 'prioritising relationship-building', and 'continuous acts of interlocking and networking'[63] are potentially relevant here. For instance, to take just one example, as several researchers point out, cultural connections might matter, in a profound way, for some young people in out-of-home care – cultural connections which might imply spirituality, family, identity, land:[64]

> the late Indigenous activist and community leader, Alf Bamblett, [who] stated that: 'Our own culture is like water for the fish. We live and breathe through it'.[65] When the child's cultural connection is weak, they

feel that something is missing, although the absence of cultural connection may not necessarily be apparent to the child. This is because, as stated by Connolly, Crichton-Hill, and Ward[66] 'culture exists below the level of consciousness, and is so deeply embedded that it escapes everyday thought'.[67]

How might our understanding and appreciation of what matters 'below the level of consciousness' be relationally explored in a co-design context, or in a qualitative research interview?

Greenaway's work[68] suggests that a specific methodological sensitivity – in the context of enduring trustful partnerships – to aspects of what matters and who matters, including those that are not readily articulated or discussed (or indeed not readily understood by researchers and practitioners), could be helpful in specific local co-design for planning during transition from out-of-home care contexts.

Shared deliberation and shared planning

Our second aspect of planning – shared deliberation in planning, in the sense discussed in Chapter 8[69] – refers to each of the informal (and formal) relationships[70] a young person values[71] and their intricate and developing roles in planning. We were aware in Chapter 9 of the repeated traumas that may have disrupted a care-leaver's sense of intersubjective experience and shared deliberation and shared planning – and the extraordinary potential for reflexive reframing and healing during emerging adulthood. And earlier in this chapter, recognition theory brought a major new perspective to bear on our understanding of the potential importance of shared aspects of planning in which recognition (in Axel Honneth's multi-layered formulation) is vital and integral, in particular for young people, such as care-leavers, who are minoritised and marginalised. Critiques of recognition theory help us also bear in mind a picture of 'complex fields in which recognition norms are continually negotiated and renegotiated, sometimes refused, occasionally affirmed, but never blind to the coloniality of the terms of recognition'.[72]

Bearing each of these points in mind, shared deliberation could refer to the potential for care-leaver shared co-design thinking with other care-leavers, professionals, and other stakeholders. Most investigators agree that co-design projects should be as social-relational as possible.[73] Co-design of the shared deliberation and shared planning aspects of transition planning would perhaps require much shared exploration, much listening and checking, much re-negotiation of norms, and perhaps several co-emerging forms of methodological sensitivity, and relying perhaps by definition on Greenaway's 'enduring trustful partnerships'?

A sense of personal time

In this third aspect of planning, a young person's sense of time might be expected to be idiosyncratic, alive and breathing, deeply personal, as a flag in the mountainside, as based in a culture, and in the 'tempo of the shape of a life'.[74]

John Burnham (2005) contrasts a client's, or family's, own particular sense of time with professional paradigms of time: 'There is, within our field, a strong preference to look to the future.'[75] He notes questions professionals might (routinely) ask, such as: 'In 5 years time where would you like to see yourself?'

But if the question doesn't fit the frame of the client (and in our studies this question would not have gone down well) what alternatives are there? Burnham suggests: 'When I mention the word future, how far ahead do you see?'[76]

On reflection, even this question implies that 'looking ahead' may be what is on the mind of the professional, but at least the question invites discussion of time.

Time and planning (for the process of specific service co-design for transition planning in specific places and times) could be decomposed and understood in its profound plurality,[77] while acknowledging real-world time constraints for participants, professionals, and stakeholders.[78] Methodological sensitivities for co-producing knowledge through enduring trustful partnerships might include,[79] in a specific local context, for instance: *young people's own accounts of time and planning being explored, as a basis for co-imagining how transition planning might have the flexibility to be appreciative of the profound plurality and diversity of temporal aspects of planning.*

Expressive emotion – the example of anger

Throughout this book we have listened out for the young person's own voiced account of what and who matters, their sense of time and planning, and accounts of shared deliberation and shared agency. We have emphasised listening to *how* these accounts or narratives are articulated – the expressive aspect of how language is used.

This can be contrasted with a designative-instrumental aspect of language.[80] While both aspects are obviously important, a key element of the research in this book has been to 'bring to light' the emotional and expressive aspects of young people's discussions about planning. Indeed, if a young person is discussing those things that matter most, and discussing those people who matter most, then of course – usually – this will be done with feeling, with voice, using expressive aspects of language.[81] Lemn Sissay's flags in the mountainside *are* expressive.

In Chapter 9 I used the examples of grief and loss in order to discuss emotions as ruptures in our lifeworlds, that is, how a background framework may be brought into question, how the implications of emotion ruptures are impossible to 'pin down', noting the two-sidedness of emotional intentionality, and the potential of emotions for revising the lifeworld. I also discussed the multiple and compounded ruptures many young people leaving care will have experienced – including *transition itself* as a potential emotion rupture; some of the very particular aspects of the experience of being in care and leaving care, such as survivalist self-reliance[82] and a raised risk of mental health and drug misuse issues; and finally the opportunity of emerging adulthood to gradually revise and re-imagine one's life, in interplay with extremely challenging and ongoing contextual inequities.

The examples, in Chapter 9, of grief and loss linked us to the relevant literatures and to the experience of young people in care, but another complex emotion that young people discussed in Chapters 3–6 was anger.

How might we recognise and respect young people's expressions of anger[83] about losses and about adversity as part of an appreciation of planning as a broader concept – as part of what and who matters, shared agency, and temporal aspects of planning? Anger may be regarded as one expressive starting point, as *one part of a multi-coloured flag in the mountainside* for co-design and co-production in the contexts of transition from out-of-home care?

Indeed, why choose to recognise anger as part of co-design for transition planning? First, it was an emotion discussed by some young people in the analyses reported in Chapters 3–6.[84] Second, anger and resentment may be regarded as articulating 'cognitively complex processes of working through the meanings of wrongdoing'.[85] Third, as Catherine Lane West-Newman points out in a key paper on anger in the legacies of empire:

> [when] collective indigenous anger meets the anger of
> non-indigenous individuals convinced that they should
> bear no personal responsibility, guilt, or shame for the
> past ... among the many things not shared in these
> societies, then, is mutual convention through which
> this just (and unjust) anger might meet in resolution ...
> No socially agreed modes exist to explore and resolve
> our anger together; it takes us to different places and
> we express it in different ways.[86]

Fourth, anger is widely understood as a potential part of post-trauma emotion processing.[87]

Part of an answer to the question of how we might include recognition of anger in co-design for transition is addressed by Martha Nussbaum with her characterisation of emotions as 'embody[ing] not simply ways of seeing an object but beliefs – often very complex – about the object'.[88] As she says:

> In order to have anger, I must have ... a complex set
> of beliefs: that some damage has occurred to me or to
> something or someone close to me; that the damage is
> not trivial but significant; that it was done by someone;
> probably that it was done willingly.[89]

This chimes with the accounts given by some young people in our studies: their anger at, and sometimes on behalf of, a birth parent; sometimes at foster parents, sometimes at institutions, sometimes at systems (see Chapters 3–6).

If we are to consider expressive language as showing and being starting points (for co-design) we might be tempted to think of expressive language as a resource: a 'motivational' resource for 'agency' – indeed for individual *and* shared planning agency[90] – a reflexive resource, a cognitive resource, a hermeneutic resource, something to be 'empowered.'[91]

Yet, and this is probably a counter-hegemonic[92] point, it is surely much more than a 'resource'. Expressive language *is* language.[93] Expressive language reflects and affects reflexivities – self-reflection, embodied reflexivity, shared deliberation and shared agency, and a sense of time – personal, shared, potentially cross-generational. And expressive language addresses power and power differentials.[94] The word 'resource' can carry instrumental connotations which do not do justice to what Charles Taylor[95] calls the expressive-constitutive nature of this hugely important part of the whole spectrum, or full shape, of human language – a part which gives rise to poetry and to literature, to punk and to rap, to demo(nstration)s and to drama, and to how we dress, arrange our hair, and express ourselves through our bodies. These are indeed 'resources', but they are also a central part of our human language, our human lives, and our human political struggles.[96] Returning to Carol Gilligan's *In a Different Voice*, and keeping young people in transition from care in mind, as Gilligan says: 'To have something to say is to be a person. But speaking depends on listening and being heard: it is an intensely relational act.'[97]

Methodologically, as a potential co-design methodological sensitivity, we cannot appreciate expressive language dispassionately[98] or in a manner that is value-free.[99] We cannot 'operationalise' these expressive accounts: our point, at least in this way of seeing things, is to try to understand the expressive feeling with which things are said by young people, in context.

Perhaps we can consider, during co-design with young people in transition from out-of-home care, an understanding and appreciation of the expression of anger, and other complex emotions, as part of our recognition of the intricate planning logics and counterlogics[100] of young people still 'processing' resentment, emotion ruptures, and compounded (intergenerational) losses.[101]

To summarise, a potential methodological sensitivity for co-producing knowledge through enduring trustful partnerships, in this context, might include: a high awareness, during co-design, that expressive and emotion-based aspects of language are key to creating a freedom of expression, and epistemic freedom,[102] particularly with young people who may have a history of having been disrespected, and not involved appropriately in decision-making and planning.[103]

This methodological sensitivity may have a range of different 'impacts on ways of knowing and doing planning',[104] one of which is its relevance to co-design research methodologies. In our own studies we used IPA[105] for many reasons, which included the potential to draw out expressive aspects of language. Narrative research methods also bring special features that allow individual and relational awareness to interview design and qualitative data analysis.[106] More traditional across-case coding-based qualitative analysis methods (focusing on designative aspects of language) may be less useful for this purpose.[107]

Thinking of different *aspects* of anger, there is much that is known about aggressive, violent, and deeply harmful interpersonal behaviour (that is, associated with anger), but perhaps less is known, and appreciated, about the experience and the 'beliefs – often very complex'[108] associated with (young people's) anger, especially in the contexts of repeated losses, family violence, racism,[109] and compounded adversity.[110] Martha Nussbaum, while discussing anger, and a belief 'that some damage has occurred to me or to something or someone close to me'[111] links this formulation to Aristotle, who 'insists that the damage must take the form of a "slight", suggesting that what is wrong with wrongdoing is always that it shows a lack of respect'.[112] Axel Honneth's careful unpacking of disrespect (to repeat – violation of the body, the denial of rights, and the denigration of ways of life[113]) brings us back, via anger, to the struggle for recognition – and the potential benefits of co-design.[114]

Conclusion

In this final chapter I have focused on young people's own voiced starting points: young people's own flags in the mountainside, what and who matters, the value placed on shared deliberation, the extraordinary plurality of time in relation to planning, and young people's own expression of feeling – including anger – about their worlds. I have asked the question: can young people's own starting points for planning also be the starting points of transition services, or potential services,[115] starting points for research and service co-design and co-production, and starting points for individual recognition, help, and support?

Cross-fertilisation of ideas between different approaches to sustainable co-design, especially those ideas focusing on minoritised and Indigenous communities, has been a focus, in particular the work of Alison Greenaway and colleagues in Aotearoa New Zealand.

In conclusion, in Chapters 3–6 of this book, eight young people in a particular space-time discuss a very wide range of personal thoughts, feelings, and logics and counterlogics about planning. This book is dedicated to *all* young people in out-of-home/state care, and in transition from care, with the hope that their voices will be heard, and acted on.[116]

Notes

Introduction

[1] Baird et al, 2021.

[2] See Chapters 1 and 4 (p 62): Danny.

[3] Hung and Appleton, 2016; Appleton, 2020; Barratt et al, 2020; Kulmala and Fomina, 2022.

[4] Bratman, 2013.

[5] Halberstam, 2003, 2005. 'This book makes the perhaps overly ambitious claim that there is such a thing as "queer time" and "queer space". Queer uses of time and space develop, at least in part, in opposition to the institutions of family, hererosexuality, and reproduction. They also develop according to other logics' (Halberstam, 2005, p 1).

[6] Samuels, 2017: 'When disabled folks talk about crip time, sometimes we just mean that we're late all the time – maybe because we need more sleep than nondisabled people, maybe because the accessible gate in the train station was locked. But other times, when we talk about crip time, we mean something more beautiful and forgiving. We mean, as my friend Margaret Price explains, we live our lives with a "flexible approach to normative time frames" like work schedules, deadlines, or even just waking and sleeping. My friend Alison Kafer says that "rather than bend disabled bodies and minds to meet the clock, crip time bends the clock to meet disabled bodies and minds." I have embraced this beautiful notion for many years, living within the embrace of a crip time that lets me define my own "normal".'

[7] Nussbaum, 2001, p 1.

[8] Archer, 2003.

[9] Hung and Appleton, 2016; Appleton et al, 2021; see Box 1.3 in this book.

[10] Box 1.1.

[11] Hiles et al, 2014; Gypen et al, 2017, Munro, 2019; Glynn, 2023; Okpych et al, 2023; Schelbe, 2023, Chapter 4; and see Chapter 1, Box 1.2 of this book.

[12] See Kulmala and Fomina, 2022, for an important recent study also finding a significant proportion of care-leavers not wishing to plan for the future.

[13] Stein, 2012; House of Commons, 2022.

[14] Barratt et al, 2020.

[15] Archer, 2003; Hung and Appleton, 2016; see Box 1.1 in Chapter 1 in this book.

[16] See Kulmala and Fomina, 2022.

[17] See Chapter 1 of this book.

[18] Galambos and Martinez, 2007; Benach et al, 2014; Schoon and Lyons-Amos, 2017; Heckhausen, 2019; Celikates et al, 2023; Patterson et al, 2023.

[19] Galambos and Martinez, 2007; Shulman and Nurmi, 2010; Arnett, 2014; Hochberg and Konner, 2020.

[20] Archer, 2003, Chapter 9.

[21] Hung and Appleton, 2016, pp 46–47.

[22] All participant names are anonymised (see Box 1.3).

[23] Example from Appleton et al, 2020, and see Hung and Appleton, 2016.

[24] See Chapter 8, this book, and see Bratman, 2013.

[25] In Kulmala and Fomina's (2022) study in North West Russia in 2018, 20 out of 43 care-leavers 'showed no or little future orientation or even refused to plan'; see also Kulmala et al, 2023, for important geographic, historic, and jurisdictional context for their study.

[26] General Assembly, United Nations, 2010; Devenney, 2017; Lemus et al, 2017; Glynn and Mayock, 2019; Munro, 2019; Brady and Gilligan, R, 2020; Dumont et al, 2022; Kulmala and Fomina, 2022; Park et al, 2020, 2022.

[27] Coulter and Collins, 2011; and see Harris and Pamukcu, 2020, and Moss, 2010, for discussions of subordination and structural inequality in public health, and the role of individual and collective agency in health.

[28] Williams and Levitt, 2007; Storm and Edwards, 2013.

[29] Jackson and Cameron, 2012; Okpych, 2012; Rios and Rocco, 2014; Okpych and Courtney, 2017; Harrison, 2020; Harrison et al, 2022.

[30] Kazemian, 2021. But also see Abrams and Terry, 2017, on 'everyday desistance' during the transition to adulthood among formerly incarcerated young people. See Weegels et al, 2020, for an account of how '"prison" and the "street" are increasingly understood to be enmeshed sites of exclusion and confinement'.

[31] Chai et al, 2021; see Alderson et al, 2020, for a pilot feasibility RCT of two behaviour change interventions to reduce substance misuse in looked after children and care-leavers.

[32] Bandura, 2006, p 164; Munford and Sanders, 2015; Brady and Gilligan, 2020; Johansson et al, 2023.

[33] Oshri et al, 2018; Cui et al, 2020.

[34] 'Few countries have well-developed care-leaving legislation. Most countries provide little aftercare beyond the age of 18, even when legislation provides for it' (Strahl et al, 2020).

[35] Stern, 1991; Kuusela, 2008; Wittgenstein, 2009 [1953] Day and Krebs, 2010; Sluga, 2011; Floyd, 2016, 2018, 2021; Read, 2020.

[36] Nussbaum, 2001, pp 1–2.

[37] "Few countries have well-developed care-leaving legislation. Most countries provide little aftercare beyond the age of 18, even when legislation provides for it" (Strahl et al, 2020).

[38] Sissay, 2019, p 173.

[39] Greenaway et al, 2022.

Notes

Chapter 1

1. Hung and Appleton, 2016; and see Chapter 4 of this book.
2. See Box 1.2 for a discussion of transition from out of home care.
3. Archer, 2003, Chapter 5; Archer, 2007, 2012.
4. Hung and Appleton, 2016; Barratt et al, 2020; Box 1.3.
5. Hung and Appleton, 2016.
6. See Archer, 2003, p 161, for definitions of each prompt.
7. Hung and Appleton, 2016.
8. Archer, 2003, p 162.
9. Hung and Appleton, 2016.
10. Hung and Appleton, 2016, and see Chapter 4 of this book.
11. Nikulina and Widom, 2013.
12. Taylor, 1985, 2016: 216–221; Bruner, 1990; Gilligan, 1993; Smith, et al, 2009; Day and Krebs, 2010; Josselson, 2013, Chapter 1; Gergen, 2014; Zimmerman, 2015; Packer, 2018, Chapter 4; Smith, 2019.
13. Sometimes referred to as 'self-reflexive'.
14. Bruner, 1990, pp 109–110, emphasis in the original. Importantly, Bruner explains that his discussion of reflexivity draws directly on Kenneth Gergen's interpretivist work on the social and historical contexts of autobiography and construction of self, and further, Bruner suggests that Gergen's own approach benefitted from Frederic Bartlett's (much) earlier work on the cultural contexts of memory (Bruner, 1990: 56–59; 108–110).
15. Archer, 2007, p 63, emphasis in the original.
16. Archer, 2003, p 103 emphasis in the original.
17. Archer, 2007, p 25.
18. Archer, 2003, p 130. See Archer 2003, 2007, 2012, and see Archer and Morgan, 2020 for bibliography.
19. Stein, 2021, p 286.
20. Mendes and Moslehuddin, 2006; Mendes and Snow, 2016.
21. Mendes and Moslehuddin, 2006.
22. Mendes and Moslehuddin, 2006, p 112.
23. Mendes and Moslehuddin, 2006, p 112; Unrau et al, 2008; As Taussig and Raviv (2022) point out: 'Because children are not randomly assigned to foster care following maltreatment, it is impossible to tease apart the impact of placement in foster care independent of the consequences of maltreatment. What we do know is that children in foster care, and those who have emancipated from care, experience high rates of cognitive, academic, physical, social, emotional and behavior problems and are more likely to experience negative outcomes.'
24. Biehal, 2014; Havlicek and Courtney, 2016; Katz et al, 2017; Carr et al, 2020; Ayaya et al, 2021; Yoshioka-Maxwell, 2022.
25. Mendes and Moslehuddin, 2006, p 112; Stein, 2021; Schelbe, 2023.
26. Mendes et al, 2012; Stein, 2012; Sulimani-Aidan, 2015; Stewart, 2016; Gypen et al, 2017; Okpych and Courtney, 2017; Pryce et al, 2017; Schofield et al, 2017; Shah et al, 2017; Refaeli et al, 2019; Harrison, 2020; Mendes

and Rogers, 2020; Sekibo, 2020; van Breda and Frimpong-Manso, 2020; van Breda, Munro et al, 2020; Glynn and Mayock, 2021; Taylor, D.J. et al, 2021; Harrison et al, 2022; Mendes et al, 2022; Stubbs et al, 2022; van Breda, 2022; Alderson et al, 2023; Glynn, 2023; Mendes et al, 2023; Okpych et al, 2023; Schelbe, 2023.

[27] Cunningham and Diversi, 2013; Havlicek et al, 2013; Gypen et al, 2017; Munro, 2019; Park and Courtney, 2022.

[28] Biehal and Wade, 1996; Wade, 2008; Mendes et al, 2012; Lee et al, 2016.

[29] For instance homelessness and mental health issues: Chikwava et al, 2022; Klodnick and Samuels, 2020. And see Schelbe, 2023, Chapter 4.

[30] Barker et al, 2014; Jackomos, 2016; Krakouer et al, 2018; O'Donnell et al, 2019; Atwool, 2020; Yi et al, 2020; Mendes et al, 2021; Chamberlain et al, 2022; Cashmore and Taylor, 2023; Lawson and Berrick, 2023; Trocme et al, 2023. To give an example of the extent of this issue in one country, Canadian research shows that First Nations children are 13 times more likely to be taken into care (following investigation of the family for child maltreatment), when compared with non-Indigenous children. Equally, in Canada, although First Nations children make up 5% of the child population, they represent 42% of children in foster care (Trocmé et al, 2023, p 94, and see Figure 5.3). In addition, in the US, it has been known for many years that Black children are disproportionately involved in the child welfare system (Dettlaff and Boyd, 2022).

[31] Sacker et al, 2021, and see Achdut et al, 2023 for a recent international review and longitudinal study in Israel of long-term employment outcomes for care-leavers.

[32] Murray et al, 2020; Batty et al, 2022; Sacker et al, 2022.

[33] Batty et al, 2022.

[34] Almquist et al, 2020; and see Wang et al, 2023; and see Steine et al, 2017.

[35] van Breda and Frimpong-Manso, 2020; van Breda and Pinkerton, 2020. See Patterson et al, 2023 for a contextual account of broader challenges for African urban youth.

[36] Frimpong-Manso, 2023.

[37] Frimpong-Manso, 2023.

[38] Bond, 2018; Theron and van Breda, 2021.

[39] Strahl et al, 2020.

[40] Mendes and Rogers, 2020; van Breda et al, 2020; see also Alderson et al, 2023; for 'Staying Put' and 'Staying Close' services in England, see House of Commons library report: *Support for Care Leavers* (2022); for a recent Australian perspective, with a particular focus on intersecting factors and housing support, see Mendes et al, 2023.

[41] van Breda et al, 2020; see also systematic review by Taylor, D.J. et al, 2021. See Refaeli et al, 2023, for an international survey of services for care leavers during COVID-19.

[42] Afsahi, 2022.

[43] Dixon et al, 2019; and see Chapter 10 on 'voice'.

[44] Fernyhough, 2016, p 3.

45   Archer, 2003.

46   Archer, 2003, Chapter 5, and see Box 1.1 in this book.

47   Hung and Appleton, 2016; Barratt et al, 2020; Appleton et al, 2021.

48   Archer, 2003, p 162.

49   Archer, 2003, p 162.

50   Archer, 2003, p 162.

51   Hung and Appleton, 2016; see Chapter 3 in this book.

52   Archer, 2003, p 142.

53   Archer, 2003, p 305.

54   Hung and Appleton, 2016.

55   In Kulmala and Fomina's (2022) study of care-leavers in North West Russia in 2018, n = 17 of 43 'planned and dreamed ahead', of whom n = 8 showed 'strong self-efficacy' and 'life course planning'. And see Matchett and Appleton, 2023.

56   Hung and Appleton, 2016.

57   Hung and Appleton, 2016, p 38.

58   Barratt et al, 2020.

59   Smith et al, 2009; Smith, 2019; Smith and Nizza, 2022; see Coxon and Smith (2021) for an interesting and engaging interview with Jonathan A. Smith, about the origins of IPA: 'I was interested in personal experience, and the meaning that experiences hold for participants' (p 46).

60   Archer, 2003.

61   Smith et al, 2009; Smith, 2019; Smith and Nizza, 2022.

62   Smith et al, 2009, pp 29–32; Smith, 2019, p 4: 'The articulation of meaning as being of a particular thing, for a particular person, within a particular context ... speaks to IPA's idiographic commitment.'

63   See Packer, 2018, chapter 3.

64   See Knight et al, 2022, for a recent example of an IPA-based qualitative interview study (n = 5) of experience of coercive medical interventions among Black Canadians with a diagnosis of first episode psychosis. And see Eatough et al, 2008.

65   Vasileiou et al, 2018.

66   Eatough et al, 2008.

67   See Tuval-Mashiach (2017) for a clear account of practical and epistemological aspects of transparency in qualitative research.

Chapter 2

1   Jonathan Smith and colleagues (2009, p 3) define double hermeneutic as follows: 'the researcher is trying to make sense of the participant trying to make sense of what is happening to them. This captures the dual role of the researcher. He/she is employing the same mental and personal skills and capacities as the participant, with whom he/she shares a fundamental property – that of being a human being.'

2   Archer, 2007, p 25.

3   Storø, 2017, p 779. See Stein, 2006.

4 Hung and Appleton, 2016.

5 Tuval-Mashiach, 2017.

6 Archer, 2003.

7 Blackburn, 1999, p 4.

8 Bandura, 2006, p 165.

9 Bandura, 2006, pp 164–165. See also Bandura's highly influential work on self-efficacy: Bandura, 1982; Refaeli et al, 2019; Kulmala and Fomina, 2022; Blakeslee et al, 2023.

10 Barratt et al, 2020.

11 Maurice Merleau-Ponty, 1962 [1945], p 98. Colin Smith translation.

12 Zaragocin and Caretta, 2021, p 1505.

13 Taylor, 2016, p 16, footnote 18, quoting Elizabeth Anscombe, 1963, p 57.

14 Van der Kolk, 2014, p 89.

15 Vandenberghe, 2005, p 234.

16 Especially in Chapter 10, with discussion of Axel Honneth's (1995, 2021) work on intersubjectivity and recognition. See also Honneth's recent discussion with colleagues on the the intersubjective, societal and political contexts of work (Celikates et al, 2023).

17 Bratman, 2014b, p 4, emphasis in the original.

18 Bratman, 2022.

19 McCrory et al, 2022; Pryce et al, 2017.

20 Bruner, 1990, pp 109–110.

21 Bruner, 1990.

22 Archer, 2003; Hung and Appleton, 2016; Barratt et al, 2020.

23 Suddendorf and Busby, 2005; Suddendorf et al, 2009.

24 D'Argembeau, 2021, p 275.

25 D'Argembeau, 2020.

26 D'Argembeau, 2020; Garcia Jimenez et al, 2023.

27 Hung and Appleton, 2016.

28 See Box 1.4. for reasons we chose to use IPA in these studies, and see Smith et al, 2009; Smith, 2019; Smith and Nizza, 2022.

29 Tuval-Mashiach, 2017.

30 Including Study 2 data in this secondary analysis would have 'increased numbers', but there are methodological differences between the two studies which would have made combining the data-sets unnecessarily complex and potentially confusing. As explained in Box 1.4. 'small numbers' (of participants) are not viewed as inherently problematic within IPA.

31 Smith et al, 2009; Smith, 2019; Smith and Nizza, 2022.

32 Smith, 2019.

33 Tarrow, 2010.

34 Floyd, 2016, p 43.

35 Smith et al, 2009, pp 101–107.

36 See Eatough et al, 2008, and Knight et al, 2022, for especially clear examples of IPA research in which there is a careful balance between idiographic and across-case theme-based analysis.

37 Hung and Appleton, 2016; Appleton, 2020.
38 Smith, 2019, p 174.
39 Floyd, 2016.
40 Appleton, 2020.
41 Smith, 2019.
42 Taylor, 1985.
43 Taylor, 2016, p 183, emphasis in the original.
44 Floyd, 2021, p 1.
45 Floyd, 2021, p 2.
46 Floyd, 2021, p 3.
47 Lock and Strong, 2010.
48 Lock and Strong, 2010, p 7.
49 Burr, 2003.
50 Bhaskar and Hartwig, 2010, p 77.
51 Bhaskar and Hartwig, 2010, p 77.
52 Hartwig, 2007, p 335.
53 See Archer and Morgan, 2020, for an interview with Margaret Archer about her career, including her role as one of the founding theorists of critical realism, and her work on drawing 'important attention to the nature of human personhood and reflexivity for any adequate account of social reality'.
54 For instance, Archer, 2003, p 40.
55 Vandenberghe, 2022, p 17.
56 Wimalasena, 2022, p 101.
57 Floyd, 2016, p 42.
58 Floyd, 2016, p 51, emphasis in the original.
59 Floyd, 2016, p 41.

Chapter 3

1   Archer, 2003, pp 161–162; Hung and Appleton, 2016.
2   Compare Biehal and Wade, 1996 on care-leavers' links with their birth families and foster families in England: 'Of those who were fostered, one quarter felt a strong identification with their foster families' (p 435). See Gwenzi, 2020, for a Zimbabwean study of care-leavers' concepts of family: 'Some participants acknowledge nonbiological definitions of family based on connectivity, co-residence, affective practices, family contact, and other forms of family display in the context of out-of-home care' (p 54).
3   There are similarities and differences with Archer's 'communicative reflexivity' (Archer, 2003, Chapter 6), the major difference being that shared deliberation (Bratman, 2014, Chapter 7; and see Chapter 8 of this book) is treated in the account given here as a form of reflexivity and planning *available to all*, rather than a 'specialised' form of reflexivity practised by only some individuals ('communicative reflexives': Archer, 2003). But I fully acknowledge the overlap/family resemblance between the two concepts, and the value of understanding Archerian communicative reflexivity for those

young care-leavers who have managed to find 'contextual continuities' in family identities (see Matchett and Appleton, 2023).

[4] Internal conversations were seen as sometimes unhelpful or ineffectual by five out of the six participants in Barratt et al's (2020) study; see Kaiser et al, 2015, and Smith, JM and Alloy, 2009 on cultural and psychological aspects of 'thinking too much' and 'rumination'.

[5] Appleton et al, 2021.

Chapter 4

[1] Kools, 1999; Samuels and Pryce, 2008; Stein, 2012; Pryce et al, 2017.

[2] Compare Kulmala and Fomina, 2022, p 211, on "'survivalist self-reliance' among those [care-leavers] who refused to plan".

[3] Wojciak et al, 2023.

[4] There is not space here to discuss implications of this for the design of interviews, and analysis of interview (and questionnaire) data, except to note that open-ended interviews have a benefit of allowing participants time and space to discuss emotionally complex matters at a point of their own choosing.

[5] Appleton et al, 2021.

[6] Schafer et al, 2004; Peguero and Hong, 2020; Salmon et al, 2022; Wiemann et al, 2023.

[7] Compare Fernyhough, 2016, p 14: 'Sometimes inner speech seems to be just like language spoken out loud; at other times it is more telegraphic and condensed, an abbreviated version of what we might utter audibly.'

[8] Appleton et al, 2021.

Chapter 5

[1] Box 1.1, this book; Hung and Appleton, 2016.

[2] Schafer et al, 2004; Peguero and Hong, 2020; Salmon et al, 2022; Wiemann et al, 2023.

[3] Shah et al, 2017.

[4] See Chapter 10, the section on 'recognition'.

[5] See Biehal and Wade, 1996; Courtney and Dworsky, 2006.

[6] Naylor et al, 2011; Teicher et al, 2022.

[7] Except in the specific form of communicative reflexivity: see Chapters 2 and 3.

[8] Barratt et al, 2020.

Chapter 6

[1] Archer, 2003, Chapter 9.

[2] Archer, 2003, pp 333–341.

[3] Burnham, 2005.

Chapter 7

[1] Srivastava and Hopwood, 2009, 2018.

[2] Srivastava and Hopwood, 2009.

[3] Bratman, 2013, p 60, my italics. Shared deliberation and shared agency are also discussed in my 2020 paper on 'Anchors for deliberation and shared deliberation: understanding planning in young adults transitioning from out of home care' (Appleton, 2020).

[4] Hung and Appleton, 2016; Barratt et al, 2020; Kulmala and Fomina, 2022.

[5] Barratt et al, 2020; and see Kulmala and Fomina (2022) on the availability of post-school education as a specific context of positive and effective short-term planning among care-leavers, some of whom were deeply sceptical of longer-term planning.

[6] See Kulmala and Fomina (2022, p 210) on irony associated with scepticism about future planning among care-leavers.

[7] Appleton et al, 2021.

[8] Honneth, 1995, Chapter 6.

[9] Archer, 2007, p 5. See van Breda, 2022, 'The contribution of supportive relationships to [residential] care-leaving outcomes: a longitudinal resilience study in South Africa', and see Okpych et al, 2023, 'Relationships that persist and protect: the role of enduring relationships on early adult outcomes among youth transitioining out of foster care [in California]'.

[10] Honneth, 1995, 2021; Glynn, 2021, 2023.

Chapter 8

[1] Quoted by Steinbeck, 2017, p 219.

[2] Steinbeck, 2017, pp 218–219. Compare Wittgenstein, 1958, pp 44–45 on 'arrang[ing] the books of a library'.

[3] Bratman, 2013.

[4] See Bratman, 2007a, 2007b, 2013, 2014a, 2014b, 2022.

[5] In D. Shoemaker (ed.) *Oxford Studies in Agency and Responsibility*, Oxford: Oxford University Press, 2013, pp 47–69.

[6] See for instance Blakeslee et al, 2022. For examples across several different professional contexts, see Introduction Notes 25–31.

[7] Bratman, 2007a, p 4.

[8] Archer, 2003.

[9] Bratman, 2022, p 5; see also: Archer, 2003, pp 39–52.

[10] See Chapter 2.

[11] Corrina, chapter 2.

[12] Danny, chapter 4; Joe, Chapter 6.

[13] Sissay, 2019, p 173.

[14] Compare Lister, 2021.

[15] Chapter 3. Also Barratt et al's (2019, pp 9–10) examples of care-leavers' apparent day-to-day and week-to-week planning in the context of strong scepticism about future-oriented planning, and Kulmala and Fomina (2022) on contextually supported short-term planning among care-leavers.

[16] Compare Ruth Lister's (2021) second edition of *Poverty*, especially chapter 5: 'Poverty and agency: from getting by to getting organized'. And see classic papers by Emirbayer and Mische, 1998, and Hitlin and Elder,

2007. See Bengtsson et al, 2020, for a Swedish longitudinal qualitative study of care-leavers' agency and time perspective. See also later in this chapter, on cross-temporal aspects of planning agency.

[17] Oxford: Oxford University Press, 2014b, p 1.

[18] See Szanto et al, 2023, for a case for a more phenomenological account of collective intentionality.

[19] See Chapter 10. For examples across several different professional contexts, see Introduction Notes 25–31.

[20] Stubbs et al, 2022.

[21] Bratman, 2022.

[22] Bratman, 2022, p 11.

[23] Appleton et al, 2021.

[24] Compare Best and Blakeslee, 2020.

[25] Bratman, 2014b, p 132.

[26] Bratman, 2022, p 20.

[27] Oxford: Oxford University Press, 2007a, p 1.

[28] Bratman, 2013, p 47.

[29] Bratman, 2013, p 47.

[30] Bratman, 2013, p 54.

[31] Bratman, 2013, p 47.

[32] Bratman, 2022, p 3.

[33] Bratman, 2013; 2022, p 6.

[34] See Millgram, 2014.

[35] See Appleton, 2020, and Chapter 9 in this book on emotion and emotional intentionality.

[36] Bratman, 2022, p 8.

[37] Ferrero, 2009.

[38] Compare Lister, 2021: chapter 5; Kulmala and Fomina, 2022; see key sociological texts on time and planning: Emirbayer and Mische, 1998; Hitlin and Elder, 2007.

[39] Compare Ellis et al, 2020, Table 1, on comparing traditional resilience models with a 'hidden talents' model – the latter emphasising skills promoted by exposure to childhood adversity.

[40] Bratman, 2007, p 205.

[41] Ratcliffe et al, 2014.

[42] See Kulmala and Fomina (2022) for a range of forms of scepticism about future orientation in their study of care-leavers in the Russian Federation.

[43] Millgram, 2014.

[44] Bratman, 2014a, p 325.

[45] Millgram, 2014, p 165.

[46] See Millgram, 2014, 2019. I am grateful to Elijah Millgram for discussion via email on planning agency.

[47] Millgram, 2014, p 171.

[48] Morton, 2011, p 569; Appleton, 2020.

[49] Morton, 2011, p 569.

[50] Morton, 2011, p 577.

Notes

51   Ratcliffe, 2014, p 10, note 28.
52   Barboza and Valentine, 2022; Davis et al, 2022.
53   Ratcliffe et al, 2014.
54   Ratcliffe et al, 2014, p 7, emphasis in the original.
55   Ratcliffe et al, 2014, p 8.
56   Herman, 1992.
57   Strahl et al, 2020.
58   Halberstam, 2003, 2005.
59   See Chapter 1 and 10 of this book, and see Afsahi, 2022.
60   Mendes and Snow, 2016; Stein, 2021.
61   Wasson, 2021, p 454.
62   Datskou, 2020.
63   Lemus et al, 2017; Devenney, 2017; Glynn and Mayock, 2019; Brady and Gilligan, 2020; Dumont et al, 2022; Kulmala and Fomina, 2022, Park et al, 2020, 2022; Matchett and Appleton, 2023.
64   See Chapter 5.
65   Floyd, 2016; Boncompagni, 2022, 2023.
66   Floyd, 2016, p 15.
67   Floyd, 2016, p 13.
68   Taylor, 1985, p 36.
69   Floyd, 2021, pp 1–7; and see Chapter 2, this book.
70   Floyd, 2021, p 1.
71   Floyd, 2021, p 2.
72   Floyd, 2016, p 66.
73   Floyd, 2016, p 66.
74   Appleton, 2020; Appleton et al, 2021.
75   See Sluga, 2011, chapter 4, 'The prodigious diversity of language games'.
76   Boncompagni, 2022, 2023.
77   Morton, 2011.
78   Read, 2018.
79   Park and Courtney, 2022; see Ogrizek et al, 2022, for a French study of incarcerated young women, born in another country, pregnant or with children, and their experience of what the authors call 'cultural hybridization' – perhaps also ' life structuring in life' (Floyd, 2016)?
80   Floyd, 2016, p 16.
81   Archer, 2003.
82   Floyd, 2016, p 43, emphasis in the original.
83   Floyd, 2016, p 43.
84   Floyd, 2016, p 46.
85   King et al, 2021.
86   Rupert Read, 2018.
87   Wittgenstein's *Blue Book*, 1958, 1969, pp 17–18.
88   Floyd, 2016, p 71.
89   Floyd, 2016, p 32.
90   Floyd, 2016, p 47.

91 Floyd, 2016, p 41, emphasis in the original.
92 Hung and Appleton, 2016, p 44.
93 Floyd, 2016, p 75.
94 Floyd, 2016, p 56.
95 See Boyes et al (eds), 2021 and compare twenty-first-century digital literacy, epistemic injustice, and discrimination (Afsahi, 2022) as historic 'replay' of social exclusions associated with literacy.
96 Floyd, 2016, p 54.
97 Floyd, 2016, p 65.
98 Floyd, 2016, p 55.
99 Floyd, 2016, p 52.

Chapter 9

1 Anger is discussed further in this book, see Chapter 10; see also Appleton et al, 2021.
2 Nussbaum, 2001.
3 Nussbaum, 2001, pp 1–3.
4 Nussbaum, 2001, p 1.
5 Compare Rupert Read, 2018, and see later in this chapter.
6 Ratcliffe, 2019, p 251.
7 Nussbaum, 2001, p 1.
8 Nussbaum, 2001, pp 20–21.
9 Nussbaum, 2001, p 27, emphasis in the original.
10 Nussbaum, 2001, p 27, emphasis in the original.
11 Nussbaum, 2001, p 28.
12 Eatough et al, 2008.
13 Nussbaum, 2001, pp 30–31, emphasis in the original.
14 Nussbaum, 2001, p 31.
15 Nussbaum, 2001, p 49.
16 Chapter 3.
17 Ratcliffe, 2019.
18 Read, 2018. There are three reasons for interweaving Read's work: first, the topic, grief, overlaps with Nussbaum's and Ratcliffe's work on emotions; second, Read uses a personal example, as does Nussbaum, to work on the philosophy of grief; third, Read, as a Wittgensteinian scholar, uses the word 'logic' carefully, in a way that overlaps with that of Juliet Floyd (see Chapter 8 of this book).
19 Ratcliffe, 2019, quoting Nussbaum, 2001, p 80.
20 Read, 2018, p 177.
21 Read, 2018, p 187.
22 Ratcliffe, 2019, p 258.
23 See Chapter 1.
24 Ratcliffe, 2019, p 266.
25 Ratcliffe, 2019, p 260.
26 Ratcliffe, 2019, p 261.

[27] Ratcliffe, 2019, p 253.

[28] For instance, transition from care?

[29] Ratcliffe, 2019, p 253, emphasis in the original.

[30] McTavish et al, 2022.

[31] Ratcliffe, 2019, p 256.

[32] Read, 2018.

[33] Read, 2018, p 181, emphasis in the original.

[34] Ratcliffe, 2019, p 264.

[35] Read, 2018, p 187.

[36] See Iyengar et al, 2014 on maternal unresolved trauma, attachment reorganisation, and potential effects of reorganisation on child attachment.

[37] Read, 2018, p 189.

[38] Ratcliffe, 2019, p 268.

[39] See Chapters 1 and 2.

[40] Galambos and Martinez, 2007; Arnett, 2014; Hochberg and Konner, 2020; van Breda and Frimpong-Manso, 2020; Haight et al, 2022.

[41] Stein, 2021.

[42] Ritunnano et al, 2023.

[43] Kong et al, 2023.

[44] Samuels and Pryce, 2008.

[45] Havlicek et al, 2013; Seker et al, 2022.

[46] Compare Havlicek and Courtney, 2016, p 120: 'it could be that providing foster youth with opportunities to make meaning of painful experiences in the past and ensuring their safety in out-of-home care ultimately offers foster youth the kind of growth that is needed to promote healthy outcomes in adulthood.'

Chapter 10

[1] Gilligan, 1993.

[2] 'Few countries have well-developed care-leaving legislation. Most countries provide little aftercare beyond the age of 18, even when legislation provides for it' (Strahl et al, 2020).

[3] I was aware of – and with colleagues had contributed to (Appleton and Minchom, 1991; Appleton 1995a, b; Appleton et al, 1997) – earlier work on participation with clients in service design and delivery, but the more recent literature on co-design is transformational.

[4] See King et al, 2022, for a recent systematic review of co-design with Indigenous young people (up to the age of 24) in health and disability contexts, and see Masterson et al, 2022, for a systematic scoping review of definitions of co-design and co-production in health and social care. Both studies draw attention to issues of definition of co-design and co-production.

[5] Greenaway et al, 2022.

[6] Lemn Sissay was Chancellor of the University of Manchester, 2015–2022, won the PEN Pinter Prize in 2019, and was appointed OBE (Poet and Playwright; For services to Literature and Charity) in the 2021 UK Queen's Birthday Honours List.

[7] Sissay, 2019.

[8] Sissay, 2019, p 173.

[9] Sissay, 2019, p 173.

[10] Sissay, 2019, p 179.

[11] Sissay, 2019, pp 178–179.

[12] Gordon, 2022, p 44, reviewing Honneth's *Recognition: A Chapter in the History of European Ideas* (2021).

[13] Honneth, 2021, p 1.

[14] Honneth, 1995, p 170.

[15] Honneth, 1995, p 179.

[16] Honneth, 1995, p 131.

[17] Honneth, 1995, p 132.

[18] Honneth, 1995, p 134.

[19] Honneth, 1995, p 134.

[20] Honneth, 1995, p 138; see Munford and Sanders, 2020.

[21] Taylor, 1994; Gutmann, 2018.

[22] Taylor, 1994; see discussion of a 'wider conception of objectivity' (Provost, 2022) – Alice Crary in conversation with Mickaëlle Provost; see Honneth et al (2010) for discussion on historic contexts of love and care and domination, and their interplay.

[23] Guttman, 2018, p 793.

[24] Honneth, 2021; and see Bankovsky and Petherbridge, 2021.

[25] A key debate has been between Nancy Fraser and Axel Honneth, 2003; for a recent in-depth account of Fraser's philosophical development, including her work on recognition, see Le Goff, 2022; for an account of social work contexts for this debate see Garrett, 2010; for a discussion on power and recognition see Honneth et al, 2010.

[26] But also see: Paulsen and Thomas, 2018; Munro, 2019; Glynn, 2021; Glynn and Mayock, 2021; Mendes et al, 2022.

[27] Simpson, 2017.

[28] Balaton-Chrimes and Stead, 2017.

[29] See Chapter 1, Box 1.2.

[30] Gone, 2022. (Quotation from paper by Joseph P. Gone, 2022, discussing North American experience, and the re-imagining of mental health services for American Indian communities.)

[31] Gordon, 2022, p 44.

[32] Törrönen and Vornanen, 2014; Lushey and Munro, 2015; Kelly et al, 2016; Dixon et al, 2019; Glynn and Mayock, 2019; Munro, 2019; Kelly et al, 2020a, 2020b; Park et al, 2020, 2022; Hoffman-Cooper, 2021; Lynch et al, 2021; Cullingworth et al, 2022; King et al, 2022; Kulmala and Fomina, 2022; Mendes et al, 2022; Alderson et al, 2023; Blakeslee et al, 2023; Krakouer, 2023. See also McTavish et al, 2022 and Cashmore et al, 2023.

[33] See Purvis et al, 2019, on conceptual origins of the term sustainability,

[34] Chambers et al, 2021.

[35] Chambers et al, 2021, p 992.

Notes

[36] Greenaway et al, 2022. See Garnett et al, 2018, for data on Indigenous peoples' management and tenure rights over a quarter of the world's land surface, and the evidence that recognising Indigenous People's rights to land, benefit-sharing and institutions is essential to meeting local and global conservation goals.

[37] Maxwell et al, 2020; and see Fisher et al, 2022, on 'ontological and epistemological broadening of "governance"'.

[38] Greenaway et al, 2022, p 439.

[39] Orlove et al, 2022; Simpson et al, 2022.

[40] Simpson et al, 2022; Ndlovu-Gatsheni, 2018; compare van Breda and Pinkerton, 2020.

[41] St John and Akama, 2022.

[42] St John and Akama, 2022, pp 22–23.

[43] Törrönen and Vornanen, 2014; Lushey and Munro, 2015; Kelly et al, 2016; Dixon et al, 2019; Glynn and Mayock, 2019; Munro, 2019; Kelly et al, 2020a, 2020b; Park et al, 2020, 2022; Hoffman-Cooper, 2021; Lynch et al, 2021; Cullingworth et al, 2022; King et al, 2022; Kulmala and Fomina, 2022; Mendes et al, 2022; Alderson et al, 2023; Blakeslee et al, 2023; Krakouer, 2023. See also McTavish et al, 2022 and Cashmore et al, 2023.

[44] Dixon et al, 2019, p 18.

[45] *Young people's* participation in co-production, in a mental health context, is now receiving detailed attention, including, relevantly for the focus of this book, 'a first paper to describe the process of co-producing a qualitative mental health research study with young people, in line with the principles of co-production' (Dewa et al, 2021, p 140). Importantly, detailed practical suggestions are made by the authors about creating safe and ethically appropriate conditions for this research. Several other key papers on co-design and co-production of mental health research, with young people as collaborators, have recently been published (see McCabe et al, 2023 for a review; and see Dewa et al, 2021; Salami et al, 2021; Wright et al, 2021; Bennett et al, 2022; Ennals et al, 2022; King et al, 2022; Viksveen et al, 2022; Culbong et al, 2023).

[46] Shimmin et al, 2017; Roche et al, 2020; Gum et al, 2023; McCabe et al, 2023.

[47] Dixon et al, 2019, p 15.

[48] Brody, 2022.

[49] Gonzalez et al, 2012; Havlicek, 2014; Knight, 2015; Riebschleger et al, 2015; Atwool, 2019, 2020. See also Sweeney et al, 2018. See Zolkos, 2019: 'The "endangered voices" of the Taiwanese victims of Japanese sexual slavery' for an account of a specific postcolonial feminist ethics of historical trauma in Taiwan.

[50] King et al, 2022.

[51] See Greenaway et al, 2022, on 'enduring trustful partnerships'.

[52] Gilmore-Bykovskyi et al, 2021; Afsahi, 2022; Diffey et al, 2022.

[53] 'Few countries have well-developed care-leaving legislation. Most countries provide little aftercare beyond the age of 18, even when legislation provides for it' (Strahl et al, 2020).

[54] Greenaway et al, 2022, p 443.

[55] Greenaway et al, 2022, Table 2.

56   Greenaway et al, 2022, p 443.

57   See Greenaway, 2022, Table 2 (emphasis added).

58   See Greenaway, 2022, Table 2 for 'model'.

59   Munro, 2019, pp 74–75; see also Munro et al, 2011; Refaeli et al, 2023.

60   Globally, most young people in transition from out-of-home care do not have access to specific aftercare services, despite UN guidance (General Assembly of the United Nations, 2010; Munro et al, 2019; Strahl et al, 2020). I therefore start with this condition, that is, no current specific aftercare services.

61   Bratman, 2013.

62   Simpson, 2017.

63   Greenaway et al, 2022, pp 433, 442, 443.

64   McDowall, 2016; Krakouer et al, 2018; Murrup-Stewart et al, 2021; Krakouer, 2023.

65   Bamblett, in Victorian Department of Justice, 2013, p 38.

66   Connolly, Crichton-Hill, and Ward, 2006, p 18.

67   Krakouer et al, 2018, p 271.

68   Greenaway et al, 2022.

69   And see Bratman, 2014b.

70   Stubbs et al, 2022; van Breda, 2022; Okpych et al, 2023.

71   Blakeslee, 2012.

72   Balaton-Chrimes and Stead, 2017, p 14.

73   Greenaway et al, 2022, for instance, in an environmental sustainability context, emphasises 'prioritising relationship-building' and 'relationships come first' (p 442); and see Bakketeig and Backe-Hansen, 2018; Mendes and Purtell, 2020; van Breda, 2022.

74   Ogden, 1997, p 637.

75   Burnham, 2005, p 14.

76   Burnham, 2005, p 14.

77   See extended discussion in Chapters 8 and 9, see earlier in this chapter, especially on 'waiting', and see King et al, 2022 on Māori temporal ontologies.

78   I am grateful to an anonymous reviewer for the point that in the reality of time-sensitive goal-oriented planning work with care-leavers, some balance must be achieved between this day-to-day reality (both for young people, and for service providers) and the wider planning and emotion issues discussed in this book.

79   Compare Greenaway et al, 2022, Table 2.

80   See Chapter 2 for a discussion of Charles Taylor's work on 'the full shape of the human linguistic capacity' (Taylor, 2016).

81   See Chapters 3–6, and Chapter 7.

82   Samuels and Pryce, 2008.

83   And other complex emotions.

84   And see Appleton et al, 2021.

85   Congdon, 2018, p 739. See Cherry, 2021, on 'why anger is essential to anti-racist struggle'.

86   West-Newman, 2004, p 204.

[87] Silove et al, 2009; Glück et al, 2017; Miles et al, 2023.

[88] Nussbaum, 2001, p 28; and see Chapter 9 of this book.

[89] Nussbaum, 2001, pp 28–29.

[90] Compare Chambers et al, 2021, on modes of co-production, including 'reframing agency': 'These cases did not seek to empower particular knowledge, but instead allowed diverse knowledge forms to be expressed.'

[91] See Chambers et al, 2021, on 'brokering power' and 'reframing power'.

[92] Read, 2020, pp 14, 85, 107, note 62.

[93] Taylor, 2016.

[94] Chambers et al, 2021.

[95] Taylor, 2016.

[96] Raza, 2022.

[97] Gilligan, 1993, p xvi.

[98] Taylor, 1985.

[99] Provost and Crary, 2022.

[100] See Chapter 8, the section entitled 'Logic'.

[101] West-Newman, 2004; Congdon, 2018; Appleton et al, 2021.

[102] Ndlovu-Gatsheni, 2018.

[103] Honneth, 1995, chapter 6; McTavish et al, 2022.

[104] Compare Greenaway et al, 2022, Table 2.

[105] See Box 1.3, and see Chapter 2 for an extended discussion of the way IPA was used in the study reported in this book. See Cooper et al, 2023, for an example of IPA in a co-design context.

[106] Josselson, 2013.

[107] Packer, 2018, chapters 2 and 3.

[108] Nussbaum, 2001, p 28.

[109] Cherry, 2021, 2023.

[110] Eatough et al, 2008.

[111] Nussbaum, 2001, p 29.

[112] Nussbaum, 2001, p 29, note 17, referring to Aristotle's *Rhetoric* 2.2 (1378a31–32). See also Spencer, 2014, p 116, on Aristotle's meaning of slighting as going 'beyond banal negligence (she didn't notice me) to entail active *belittlement* or *diminution* of one's sense of self and standing in the world' (emphasis in the original).

[113] And see Honneth, 1995, chapter 6.

[114] The examples of co-design in this chapter have focused on transition planning in *social care*, but, as indicated in the Introduction (and see Munro, 2019, on care leavers' rights to access a range of services), there are other fundamental participatory (planning) contexts for young people experiencing compounded adversity and minoritisation such as physical health (shared decision-making and self-management in chronic illness, Sharpe et al, 2021), or co-designing a project in young people's mental health care – see earlier in this chapter, or equivalent *planning-rich co-design contexts* in post-school education, criminal justice, housing, and so on (see Introduction endnotes 26-31).

[115] Strahl et al, 2020.

[116] Dixon et al, 2019.

References

Abrams, L.S., and Terry, D. (2017) *Everyday Desistance: The Transition to Adulthood among Formerly Incarcerated Youth*, New Brunswick, NJ and London: Rutgers University Press.

Achdut, N., Benbenishty, R., and Zeira, A. (2023) 'Labor market position among care leavers and their matched peers: a longitudinal comparative study', *Child Abuse & Neglect*, 145: 106406.

Afsahi, A. (2022) 'Towards a principle of most-deeply affected', *Philosophy & Social Criticism*, 48(1): 40–61.

Alderson, H., Kaner, E., McColl, E., Howel, D., Fouweather, T., McGovern, R., et al (2020) 'A pilot feasibility randomised controlled trial of two behaviour change interventions compared to usual care to reduce substance misuse in looked after children and care leavers aged 12–20 years: the SOLID study', *PLOS One*, 15(9): e0238286.

Alderson, H., Smart, D., Kerridge, G., Currie, G., Johnson, R., Kaner, E., et al (2023) 'Moving from "what we know works" to "what we do in practice": an evidence overview of implementation and diffusion of innovation in transition to adulthood for care experienced young people', *Child & Family Social Work*, 23(3): 869–896.

Almquist, Y.B., Rojas, Y., Vinnerljung, B. and Brännström, L. (2020) 'Association of child placement in out-of-home care with trajectories of hospitalization because of suicide attempts from early to late adulthood', *JAMA network open*, 3(6): e206639.

Anscombe, E. (1963) *Intention* (2nd edn), Cambridge, MA: Harvard University Press.

Appleton, P. (1995a) 'Parental participation in child development centres', in N. Spencer (ed.) *Progress in Community Child Health, Volume 1*, Edinburgh: Churchill Livingstone, pp 69–80.

Appleton, P. (1995b) 'Young people with a disability: aspects of social empowerment', in C. Cloke and M. Davies (eds) *Participation and Empowerment in Child Protection*, London: Pitman Publishing, pp 104–119.

Appleton, P. (2020) 'Anchors for deliberation and shared deliberation: understanding planning in young adults transitioning from out-of-home care', *Qualitative Social Work*, 19(5–6): 1130–1146.

Appleton, P.L., and Minchom, P.E. (1991) 'Models of parent partnership and child development centres', *Child: Care, Health and Development*, 17(1): 27–38.

Appleton, P.L., Böll, V., Everett, J.M., Kelley, A.M., Meredith, K.H., and Payne, T.G. (1997) 'Beyond child development centres: care coordination for children with disabilities', *Child: Care, Health and Development*, 23(1): 29–40.

Appleton, P., Hung, I., and Barratt, C. (2021) 'Internal conversations, self-reliance and social support in emerging adults transitioning from out-of-home care: an interpretative phenomenological study', *Clinical Child Psychology and Psychiatry*, 26(3): 882–893.

Archer, M.S. (2003) *Structure, Agency and the Internal Conversation*, Cambridge: Cambridge University Press.

Archer, M.S. (2007) *Making Our way Through the World: Human Reflexivity and Social Mobility*, Cambridge: Cambridge University Press.

Archer, M.S. (2012) *The Reflexive Imperative in Late Modernity*, Cambridge: Cambridge University Press.

Archer, M.S., and Morgan, J. (2020) 'Contributions to realist social theory: an interview with Margaret S. Archer', *Journal of Critical Realism*, 19(2): 179–200.

Arnett, J. (2014) *Emerging Adulthood: The Winding Road from the Late Teens through the Twenties* (2nd edn), Oxford: Oxford University Press.

Atwool, N. (2019) 'Challenges of operationalizing trauma-informed practice in child protection services in New Zealand', *Child & Family Social Work*, 24(1): 25–32.

Atwool, N. (2020) 'Transition from care: are we continuing to set care leavers up to fail in New Zealand?', *Children and Youth Services Review*, vol. 113, doi: 10.1016/j.childyouth.2020.104995.

Ayaya, S., DeLong, A., Embleton, L., Ayuku, D., Sang, E., Hogan, J., et al (2021) 'Prevalence, incidence and chronicity of child abuse among orphaned, separated, and street-connected children and adolescents in western Kenya: what is the impact of care environment?', *Child Abuse & Neglect*, 139: 104920.

Baird, H.M., Webb, T.L., Sirois, F.M., and Gibson-Miller, J. (2021) 'Understanding the effects of time perspective: a meta-analysis testing a self-regulatory framework', *Psychological Bulletin*, 147(3): 233.

Bakketeig, E., and Backe-Hansen, E. (2018) 'Agency and flexible support in transition from care: learning from the experiences of a Norwegian sample of care leavers doing well', *Nordic Social Work Research*, 8(sup1): 30–42.

Balaton-Chrimes, S. and Stead, V. (2017) 'Recognition, power and coloniality', *Postcolonial Studies*, 20: 1–17.

Bankovsky, M., and Petherbridge, D. (2021) 'Recognition beyond French–German divides: engaging Axel Honneth', *Critical Horizons*, 22(1): 1–4.

Bandura, A. (1982) 'Self-efficacy mechanism in human agency', *American Psychologist*, 37(2): 122–147.

Bandura, A. (2006) 'Toward a psychology of human agency', *Perspectives on Psychological Science*, 1(2): 164–180.

Barboza, G.E. and Valentine, R. (2022) 'A network analysis of post-traumatic stress among youth aging out of the foster care system', *Children and Youth Services Review*, 140: 106589.

Barker, B., Alfred, G.T., and Kerr, T. (2014) 'An uncaring state? The overrepresentation of First Nations children in the Canadian child welfare system', *Canadian Medical Association Journal*, 186(14): E533–E535.

Barratt, C., Appleton, P., and Pearson, M. (2020) 'Exploring internal conversations to understand the experience of young adults transitioning out of care', *Journal of Youth Studies*, 23(7): 869–885.

Batty, G.D., Kivimäki, M., and Frank, P. (2022) 'State care in childhood and adult mortality: a systematic review and meta-analysis of prospective cohort studies', *The Lancet Public Health*, 7(6): e504–e514.

Benach, J., Vives, A., Amable, M., Vanroelen, C., Tarafa, G., and Muntaner, C. (2014) 'Precarious employment: understanding an emerging social determinant of health', *Annual Review of Public Health*, 35: 229–253.

Bengtsson, M., Sjöblom, Y., and Öberg, P. (2020) 'Transitional patterns when leaving care: care leavers' agency in a longitudinal perspective', *Children and Youth Services Review*, 118: 105486.

Bennett, V., Gill, C., Miller, P., Wood, A., Bennett, C., Ypag, N., and Singh, I. (2022) 'Co-production to understand online help-seeking for young people experiencing emotional abuse and neglect: building capabilities, adapting research methodology and evaluating involvement and impact', *Health Expectations*, 25(6): 3143–3163.

Best, J.I., and Blakeslee, J.E. (2020) 'Perspectives of youth aging out of foster care on relationship strength and closeness in their support networks', *Children and Youth Services Review*, 108: 104626.

Bhaskar, R., and Hartwig, M. (2010) *The Formation of Critical Realism: A Personal Perspective*, London: Routledge.

Biehal, N. (2014) 'Maltreatment in foster care: a review of the evidence', *Child Abuse Review*, 23(1): 48–60.

Biehal, N., and Wade, J. (1996) 'Looking back, looking forward: care leavers, families and change', *Children and Youth Services Review*, 18(4–5): 425–445.

Blackburn, S. (1999) *Think: A Compelling Introduction to Philosophy*, Oxford: Oxford University Press.

Blakeslee, J. (2012) 'Expanding the scope of research with transition-age foster youth: applications of the social network perspective', *Child & Family Social Work*, 17(3): 326–336.

Blakeslee, J., Miller, R., and Uretsky, M. (2022) 'Efficacy of the Project Futures self-determination coaching model for college students with foster care backgrounds and mental health challenges', *Children and Youth Services Review*, 138: 106507.

Blakeslee, J.E., Kothari, B.H., and Miller, R.A. (2023) 'Intervention development to improve foster youth mental health by targeting coping self-efficacy and help-seeking', *Children and Youth Services Review*, 144: 106753.

Boncompagni, A. (2022) *Wittgenstein on Forms of Life,* Cambridge: Cambridge University Press.

Boncompagni, A. (2023) 'Forms of life and linguistic change: the case of trans communities', *Philosophies*, 8(3): 50.

Bond, S. (2018) 'Care-leaving in South Africa: an international and social justice perspective', *Journal of International and Comparative Social Policy*, 34(1): 76–90.

Boyes, P.J., Steele, P.M., and Astoreca, N.E. (eds) (2021) *The Social and Cultural Contexts of Historic Writing Practices*, Oxford: Oxbow Books.

Brady, E., and Gilligan, R. (2020) 'The role of agency in shaping the educational journeys of care-experienced adults: insights from a life course study of education and care', *Children & Society*, 34(2): 121–135.

Bratman, M.E. (2007a) *Structures of Agency*, Oxford: Oxford University Press.

Bratman, M.E. (2007b) 'Anchors for deliberation', in C. Lumer and S. Nannini (eds) *Intentionality, Deliberation and Autonomy: The Action-Theoretic Basis of Practical Philosophy*, Aldershot: Aldgate, pp 187–205.

Bratman, M.E. (2013) 'The fecundity of planning agency', in D. Shoemaker (ed.) *Oxford Studies in Agency and Responsibility*, Oxford: Oxford University Press, pp 47–69.

Bratman, M.E. (2014a) 'Rational and social agency: reflections and replies', in M. Vargas and G. Yaffe (eds) *Rational and Social Agency: The Philosophy of Michael Bratman*, Oxford: Oxford University Press, pp 294–335.

Bratman, M.E. (2014b) *Shared Agency: A Planning Theory of Acting Together*, Oxford: Oxford University Press.

Bratman, M.E. (2022) *Shared and Institutional Agency: Toward a Planning Theory of Human Practical Organization*, Oxford: Oxford University Press.

Brody, H. (2022) *Landscapes of Silence: From Childhood to the Arctic*, London: Faber.

Bruner, J. (1990) *Acts of Meaning*, Cambridge, MA: Harvard University Press.

Burnham, J. (2005) 'Relational reflexivity: a tool for socially constructing therapeutic relationships', in C. Flaskas, B. Mason, and A. Perlesz (eds) *The Space Between: Experience, Context and Process in the Therapeutic Relationship*, London: Karnac, pp 1–19.

Burr, V. (2003) *Social Constructionism* (2nd edn), London: Routledge.

Carr, A., Duff, H., and Craddock, F. (2020) 'A systematic review of the outcome of child abuse in long-term care', *Trauma, Violence, & Abuse*, 21(4): 660–677.

Cashmore, J., and Taylor, N. (2023) 'Child protection in Australia and New Zealand: an overview of systems', in J.D. Berrick, N. Gilbert, and M. Skivenes (eds) *The Oxford Handbook of Child Protection Systems*, Oxford: Oxford University Press, pp 25–46.

Cashmore, J., Kong, P., and McLaine, M. (2023) 'Children's participation in care and protection decision-making matters', *Laws*, 12(3): 49.

Celikates, R., Honneth, A., and Jaeggi, R. (2023) 'The working sovereign: a conversation with Axel Honneth', *Journal of Classical Sociology*, 23(3): 318–338. doi: 1468795X231170980.

Chai, D., Rosic, T., Panesar, B., Sanger, N., van Reekum, E.A., Marsh, D.C., et al (2021) 'Patient-reported goals of youths in Canada receiving medication-assisted treatment for opioid use disorder', *JAMA Network Open*, 4(8): e2119600–e2119600.

Chamberlain, C., Gray, P., Bennet, D., Elliott, A., Jackomos, M., Krakouer, J., and Langton, M. (2022) 'Supporting Aboriginal and Torres Strait Islander families to stay together from the start (SAFeST Start): urgent call to action to address crisis in infant removals', *Australian Journal of Social Issues*, 57(2): 252–273.

Chambers, J.M., Wyborn, C., Ryan, M.E., Reid, R.S., Riechers, M., Serban, A., et al (2021) 'Six modes of co-production for sustainability', *Nature Sustainability*, 4(11): 983–996.

Cherry, M. (2021) *The Case for Rage: Why Anger Is Essential to Anti-Racist Struggle*, Oxford: Oxford University Press.

Cherry, M. (2023) 'The nature and normativity of anger types: a response to critics', *The Southern Journal of Philosophy*, 61(2): 399–407.

Chikwava, F., O'Donnell, M., Ferrante, A., Pakpahan, E., and Cordier, R. (2022) 'Patterns of homelessness and housing instability and the relationship with mental health disorders among young people transitioning from out-of-home care: retrospective cohort study using linked administrative data', *PLOS One*, 17(9): e0274196.

Congdon, M. (2018) 'Creative resentments: the role of emotions in moral change', *The Philosophical Quarterly*, 68(273): 739–757.

Connolly, M., Crichton-Hill, Y., and Ward, T. (2006) *Culture and Child Protection: Reflexive Responses*, London: Jessica Kingsley Publishers.

Cooper, K., Mandy, W., Butler, C., and Russell, A. (2023) 'Phenomenology of gender dysphoria in autism: a multiperspective qualitative analysis', *Journal of Child Psychology and Psychiatry*, 64(2): 265–276.

Coulter, A., and Collins, A. (2011) *Making Shared Decision-Making a Reality: No Decision about Me, without Me*, London: King's Fund.

Courtney, M.E., and Dworsky, A. (2006) 'Early outcomes for young adults transitioning from out-of-home care in the USA', *Child & Family Social Work*, 11(3): 209–219.

Coxon, A., and Smith, J.A. (2021) 'The person becomes the universe of exploration', *The Psychologist*, 34 (September): 46–49.

Culbong, H., Ramirez-Watkins, A., Anderson, S., Culbong, T., Crisp, N., Pearson, G., et al (2023) ' "Ngany Kamam, I speak truly": first-person accounts of Aboriginal youth voices in mental health service reform', *International Journal of Environmental Research and Public Health*, 20(11): 6019.

Cui, Z., Oshri, A., Liu, S., Smith, E.P., and Kogan, S.M. (2020) 'Child maltreatment and resilience: the promotive and protective role of future orientation', *Journal of Youth and Adolescence*, 49(10): 2075–2089.

Cullingworth, J., Brunner, R., and Watson, N. (2022) 'Not the usual suspects: creating the conditions for and implementing co-production with marginalised young people in Glasgow', *Public Policy and Administration*. doi: 09520767221140439.

Cunningham, M.J., and Diversi, M. (2013) 'Aging out: youths' perspectives on foster care and the transition to independence', *Qualitative Social Work*, 12(5): 587–602.

D'Argembeau, A. (2020) 'Zooming in and out on one's life: autobiographical representations at multiple time scales', *Journal of Cognitive Neuroscience*, 32(11): 2037–2055.

D'Argembeau, A. (2021) 'Memory, future thinking, and the self. In honour of Martial Van Der Linden', *Psychologica Belgica*, 61(1): 274–283.

Datskou, E. (2020) 'Queer temporalities: resisting family, reproduction and lineage in Emily Brontë's *Wuthering Heights*', *Brontë Studies*, 45(2): 132–143.

Davis, R.S., Halligan, S.L., Meiser-Stedman, R., Elliott, E., Ward, G., and Hiller, R. M. (2022) 'A longitudinal investigation of the relationship between trauma-related cognitive processes and internalising and externalising psychopathology in young people in out-of-home care', *Research on Child and Adolescent Psychopathology*, 51(4): 485–496.

Day, W., and Krebs, V. (eds) (2010) *Seeing Wittgenstein Anew*, Cambridge: Cambridge University Press.

Dettlaff, A.J., Boyd, R. (2022) 'The causes and consequences of racial disproportionality and disparities', in R.D. Krugman and J.E. Korbin (eds) *Handbook of Child Maltreatment*, Cham: Springer, pp 221–237.

Devenney, K. (2017) 'Pathway planning with unaccompanied young people leaving care: biographical narratives of past, present, and future', *Child & Family Social Work*, 22(3): 1313–1321.

Dewa, L.H., Lawrence-Jones, A., Crandell, C., Jaques, J., Pickles, K., Lavelle, M., et al (2021) 'Reflections, impact and recommendations of a co-produced qualitative study with young people who have experience of mental health difficulties', *Health Expectations*, 24: 134–146.

Diffey, J., Wright, S., Uchendu, J.O., Masithi, S., Olude, A., Juma, D.O., et al (2022) '"Not about us without us" – the feelings and hopes of climate-concerned young people around the world', *International Review of Psychiatry*, 34(5): 499–509.

Dixon, J., Ward, J., and Blower, S. (2019) '"They sat and actually listened to what we think about the care system": the use of participation, consultation, peer research and co-production to raise the voices of young people in and leaving care in England', *Child Care in Practice*, 25(1): 6–21.

Dumont, A., Lanctôt, N., and Paquette, G. (2022) '"I had a shitty past; I want a great future.": hopes and fears of vulnerable adolescent girls aging out of care', *Children and Youth Services Review*, 134: 106374.

Eatough, V., Smith, J.A., and Shaw, R. (2008) 'Women, anger, and aggression: an interpretative phenomenological analysis', *Journal of Interpersonal Violence*, 23(12): 1767–1799.

Ellis, B.J., Abrams, LS., Masten, A.S., Sternberg, R.J., Tottenham, N. and Frankenhuis, W.E. (2020) 'Hidden talents in harsh environments', *Development and Psychopathology*, 34(1): 95–113.

Emirbayer, M., and Mische, A. (1998) 'What is agency?', *American Journal of Sociology*, 103(4): 962–1023.

Ennals, P., Lessing, K., Spies, R., Egan, R., Hemus, P., Droppert, K., et al (2022) 'Co-producing to understand what matters to young people living in youth residential rehabilitation services', *Early Intervention in Psychiatry*, 16(7): 782–791.

Fernyhough, C. (2016) *The Voices Within: The History and Science of How We Talk to Ourselves,* London: Profile Books.

Ferrero, L. (2009) 'What good is a diachronic will?', *Philosophical Studies*, 144(3): 403–430.

Fisher, K., Makey, L., Macpherson, E., Paul, A., Rennie, H., Talbot-Jones, J., and Jorgensen, E. (2022) 'Broadening environmental governance ontologies to enhance ecosystem-based management in Aotearoa New Zealand', *Maritime Studies*, 21(4): 609–629.

Floyd, J. (2016) 'Chains of life: Turing, *Lebensform*, and the emergence of Wittgenstein's later style', *Nordic Wittgenstein Review*, 5(2): 7–89.

Floyd, J. (2018) 'Aspects of aspects', in H. Sluga and D. Stern (eds) *The Cambridge Companion to Wittgenstein* (2nd edn), Cambridge: Cambridge University Press, pp 361–388.

Floyd, J. (2021) *Wittgenstein's Philosophy of Mathematics*, Cambridge: Cambridge University Press.

Fraser, N., and Honneth, A. (2003) *Redistribution or Recognition?: A Political-Philosophical Exchange*, London: Verso.

Frimpong-Manso (2023) 'Residential care-leaving in the Global South: a review of the current literature', in S. Mozes and M. Israelashvili (eds) *Youth without Family to Lean On: Global Challenges and Local Interventions*, London: Routledge, pp 165–178.

Galambos, N.L., and Martínez, M.L. (2007) 'Poised for emerging adulthood in Latin America: a pleasure for the privileged', *Child Development Perspectives*, 1(2): 109–114.

Garcia Jimenez, C., Mazzoni, G., and D'Argembeau, A. (2023) 'Repeated simulation increases belief in the future occurrence of uncertain events', *Memory & Cognition*, 51(7): 1593–1606.

Garnett, S.T., Burgess, N.D., Fa, J.E., Fernández-Llamazares, Á., Molnár, Z., Robinson, C.J., et al (2018) 'A spatial overview of the global importance of Indigenous lands for conservation', *Nature Sustainability*, 1(7): 369–374.

Garrett, P.M. (2010) 'Recognizing the limitations of the political theory of recognition: Axel Honneth, Nancy Fraser and social work', *British Journal of Social Work*, 40(5): 1517–1533.

General Assembly of the United Nations (2010) *Guidelines for the Alternative Care of Children*, Resolution/64/142.

Gergen, K.J. (2014) 'Pursuing excellence in qualitative inquiry', *Qualitative Psychology*, 1(1): 49.

Gilligan, C. (1982, 1993) *In a Different Voice: Psychological Theory and Women's Development,* London: Harvard University Press.

Gilmore-Bykovskyi, A., Jackson, J.D., and Wilkins, C.H. (2021) 'The urgency of justice in research: beyond COVID-19', *Trends in Molecular Medicine*, 27(2): 97–100.

Glück, T.M., Knefel, M., and Lueger-Schuster, B. (2017) 'A network analysis of anger, shame, proposed ICD-11 post-traumatic stress disorder, and different types of childhood trauma in foster care settings in a sample of adult survivors', *European Journal of Psychotraumatology*, 8(suppl. 3): 1372543.

Glynn, N. (2021) 'Understanding care leavers as youth in society: a theoretical framework for studying the transition out of care', *Children and Youth Services Review*, 121: 105829.

Glynn, N. (2023). *Youth Transitions Out of State Care: Being Recognized as Worthy of Care, Respect, and Support*, Bingley: Emerald Publishing Limited.

Glynn, N. and Mayock, P. (2019) ' "I've changed so much within a year": care leavers' perspectives on the aftercare planning process', *Child Care in Practice*, 25(1): 79–98.

Glynn, N., and Mayock, P. (2021) 'Housing after care: understanding security and stability in the transition out of care through the lenses of liminality, recognition and precarity', *Journal of Youth Studies*, 26(1): 80–97.

Gone, J.P. (2022) 'Re-imagining mental health services for American Indian communities: centering Indigenous perspectives', *American Journal of Community Psychology*, 69(3–4): 257–268.

Gonzalez, R., Cameron, C., and Klendo, L. (2012) 'The therapeutic family model of care: an attachment and trauma informed approach to transitional planning', *Developing Practice: The Child, Youth and Family Work Journal*, 32: 13–23.

Gordon, Peter E. (2022) 'In search of recognition', *The New York Review*, 23 June (Review of Axel Honneth, 2020, *Recognition: A Chapter in the History of European Ideas*, Cambridge: Cambridge University Press).

Greenaway, A., Hohaia, H., Le Heron, E., Le Heron, R., Grant, A., Diprose, G., et al (2022) 'Methodological sensitivities for co-producing knowledge through enduring trustful partnerships', *Sustainability Science*, 17: 443–447.

Gum, A.M., Goldsworthy, M., Guerra, L., Salloum, A., Grau, M., Gottstein, S., et al (2023) 'Trauma-informed patient and public-engaged research: development and evaluation of an online training programme', *Health Expectations*, 26(1): 388–398.

Gutmann, A. (2018) 'The power of recognition: when Charles Taylor parsed personal identity', *Philosophy & Social Criticism*, 44(7): 793–795.

Gwenzi, G.D. (2020) 'Constructing the meaning of "family" in the context of out-of-home care: an exploratory study on residential care leavers in Harare, Zimbabwe', *Emerging Adulthood*, 8(1): 54–63.

Gypen, L., Vanderfaeillie, J., De Maeyer, S., Belenger, L. and Van Holen, F. (2017) 'Outcomes of children who grew up in foster care: systematic-review', *Children and Youth Services Review*, 76: 74–83.

Haight, W., Cho, M., Soffer-Elnekave, R., Nashandi, N.J. and Suleiman, J. (2022) 'Moral injury experienced by emerging adults with child welfare histories in developmental and sociocultural contexts: "I knew the system was broken"', *Children and Youth Services Review*, 139: 106537.

Halberstam, J. (2003) 'What's that smell? Queer temporalities and subcultural lives', *International Journal of Cultural Studies*, 6(3): 313–333.

Halberstam, J. (2005) *In a Queer Time and Place: Transgender Bodies, Subcultural Lives,* New York and London: New York University Press.

Harris, A.P., and Pamukcu, A. (2020) 'The civil rights of health: a new approach to challenging structural inequality', *UCLA Law Review*, 67: 758–832.

Harrison, N. (2020) 'Patterns of participation in higher education for care-experienced students in England: why has there not been more progress?', *Studies in Higher Education*, 45(9): 1986–2000.

Harrison, N., Baker, Z., and Stevenson, J. (2022) 'Employment and further study outcomes for care-experienced graduates in the UK', *Higher Education*, 83: 357–378.

Hartwig, M. (ed.) (2007) *Dictionary of Critical Realism*, London: Routledge.

Havlicek, J. (2014) 'Maltreatment histories of foster youth exiting out-of-home care through emancipation: a latent class analysis', *Child Maltreatment*, 19(3–4): 199–208.

Havlicek, J., and Courtney, M.E. (2016) 'Maltreatment histories of aging out foster youth: a comparison of official investigated reports and self-reports of maltreatment prior to and during out-of-home care', *Child Abuse & Neglect*, 52: 110–122.

Havlicek, J.R., Garcia, A.R., and Smith, D.C. (2013) 'Mental health and substance use disorders among foster youth transitioning to adulthood: past research and future directions', *Children and Youth Services Review*, 35(1): 194–203.

Herman, J.L. (1992) *Trauma and Recovery,* New York: Basic Books.

Hiles, D., Moss, D., Thorne, L., Wright, J., and Dallos, R. (2014) ' "So what am I?" – multiple perspectives on young people's experience of leaving care', *Children and Youth Services Review*, 41: 1–15.

Hitlin, S., and Elder Jr, G.H. (2007) 'Time, self, and the curiously abstract concept of agency', *Sociological Theory*, 25(2): 170–191.

Hochberg, Z.E., and Konner, M. (2020) 'Emerging adulthood, a pre-adult life-history stage', *Frontiers in Endocrinology*, 10: 918.

Hoffman-Cooper, A.E. (2021) 'From foster youth to foster scholar: suggestions for emancipatory research practices', *Children and Youth Services Review*, 120: 105752.

Honneth, A. (1995) *The Struggle for Recognition: The Moral Grammar of Social Conflicts*, Cambridge: Polity Press.

Honneth, A. (2021) *Recognition: A Chapter in the History of European Ideas*, Cambridge: Cambridge University Press.

Honneth, A., Allen, A., and Cooke, M. (2010) 'A conversation between Axel Honneth, Amy Allen and Maeve Cooke, Frankfurt am Main, 12 April 2010', *Journal of Power*, 3(2): 153–170.

House of Commons Library (2022) *Support for Care Leavers*, Research Briefing Paper.

Hung, I., and Appleton, P. (2016) 'To plan or not to plan: the internal conversations of young people leaving care', *Qualitative Social Work*, 15(1): 35–54.

Iyengar, U., Kim, S., Martinez, S., Fonagy, P., and Strathearn, L. (2014) 'Unresolved trauma in mothers: intergenerational effects and the role of reorganization', *Frontiers in Psychology*, 5: 966.

Jackomos, A. (2016) 'Being strong in Aboriginal identity and culture protects young people leaving care', *Parity*, 29(1): 14–15.

Jackson, S., and Cameron, C. (2012) 'Leaving care: looking ahead and aiming higher', *Children and Youth Services Review*, 34(6): 1107–1114.

Johansson, H., Sjöblom, Y., Höjer, I., Gilligan, R., Arnau-Sabatés, L., Pazlarová, H., et al (2023) 'Exploring care leavers' agency in achieving entry into the world of work: a cross-national study in six countries', *International Journal of Social Welfare*. doi: 10.1111/ijsw.12603.

Josselson, R. (2013) *Interviewing for Qualitative Inquiry: A Relational Approach,* London: The Guilford Press.

Kaiser, B.N., Haroz, E.E., Kohrt, B.A., Bolton, P.A., Bass, J.K. and Hinton, D.E. (2015) '"Thinking too much": a systematic review of a common idiom of distress', *Social Science & Medicine*, 147: 170–183.

Katz, C., Courtney, M. and Novotny, E. (2017) 'Pre-foster care maltreatment class as a predictor of maltreatment in foster care', *Child and Adolescent Social Work Journal*, 34(1): 35–49.

Kazemian, L. (2021) 'Pathways to desistance from crime among juveniles and adults: applications to criminal justice policy and practice', *Desistance from Crime*, National Institute of Justice, US Department of Justice, Washington, DC.

Kelly, B., Dixon, J. and Incarnato, M. (2016) 'Peer research with young people leaving care: reflections from research in England, Northern Ireland and Argentina', in P. Mendes and P. Snow (eds) *Young People Transitioning from Out-of-Home Care*. London: Palgrave, pp 221–240.

Kelly, B., Friel, S., McShane, T., Pinkerton, J., and Gilligan, E. (2020a) '"I haven't read it, I've lived it!" The benefits and challenges of peer research with young people leaving care', *Qualitative Social Work*, 19(1): 108–124.

Kelly, B., van Breda, A.D., Santin, O., Bekoe, J., Bukuluki, P., Chereni, A., et al (2020b) *Building Positive Futures: A Pilot Study on Leaving Care in Africa – Youth Report*. Queen's University Belfast.

King, C., Bennett, M., Fulford, K.W., Clarke, S., Gillard, S., Bergqvist, A., and Richardson, J. (2021) 'From preproduction to coproduction: COVID-19, whiteness, and making black mental health matter', *The Lancet Psychiatry*, 8(2): 93–95.

King, P.T., Cormack, D., Edwards, R., Harris, R., and Paine, S.J. (2022) 'Co-design for indigenous and other children and young people from priority social groups: a systematic review', *SSM-Population Health*, 18: 101077.

King, P.T., Cormack, D., Harris, R., Paine, S.J., and McLeod, M. (2022) '"Never-ending beginnings": a qualitative literature review of Māori temporal ontologies', *Kōtuitui: New Zealand Journal of Social Sciences Online*, 18(3): 252–267.

Klodnick, V.V., and Samuels, G.M. (2020) 'Building home on a fault line: aging out of child welfare with a serious mental health diagnosis', *Child & Family Social Work*, 25(3): 704–713.

Knight, C. (2015) 'Trauma-informed social work practice: practice considerations and challenges', *Clinical Social Work Journal*, 43(1): 25–37.

Knight, S., Jarvis, G.E., Ryder, A.G., Lashley, M., and Rousseau, C. (2022) '"It just feels like an invasion": Black first-episode psychosis patients' experiences with coercive intervention and its influence on help-seeking behaviours', *Journal of Black Psychology*, 49(2): 200–235. doi: 00957984221135377.

Kong, C., Campbell, M., Kpobi, L., Swartz, L., and Atuire, C. (2023) 'The hermeneutics of recovery: facilitating dialogue between African and Western mental health frameworks', *Transcultural Psychiatry*, 60(3): 428–442.

Kools, S. (1999) 'Self-protection in adolescents in foster care', *Journal of Child and Adolescent Psychiatric Nursing*, 12(4): 139–152.

Krakouer, J. (2023) 'Journeys of culturally connecting: Aboriginal young people's experiences of cultural connection in and beyond out-of-home care', *Child & Family Social Work*, 28(3): 822–832.

Krakouer, J., Wise, S., and Connolly, M. (2018) ' "We live and breathe through culture": conceptualising cultural connection for Indigenous Australian children in out-of-home care', *Australian Social Work*, 71(3): 265–276.

Kulmala, M., and Fomina, A. (2022) 'Planning for the future: future orientation, agency and self-efficacy of young adults leaving care in the Russian Arctic', in F. Stammler and R. Toivanen (eds) *Young People, Wellbeing and Placemaking in the Arctic*, London: Routledge, pp 196–221.

Kulmala, M., Jäppinen, M., and Chernova, Z. (2023) 'Reforming Russia's child protection system: from institutional to family care', in J.D. Berrick, N. Gilbert and M. Skivenes (eds) *The Oxford Handbook of Child Protection Systems*, Oxford: Oxford University Press, pp 877–899.

Kuusela, O. (2008) *The Struggle against Dogmatism: Wittgenstein and the Concept of Philosophy*, London: Harvard University Press.

Lawson, J., and Berrick, J.D. (2023) 'Child protection in the United States', in J.D. Berrick, N. Gilbert, and M. Skivenes (eds) *The Oxford Handbook of Child Protection Systems*, Oxford: Oxford University Press, pp 381–396.

Lee, B.R., Cole, A.R., and Munson, M.R. (2016) 'Navigating family roles and relationships: system youth in the transition years', *Child & Family Social Work*, 21(4): 442–451.

Le Goff, A. (2022) 'From a theory of justice to a critique of capitalism: how Nancy Fraser revitalizes social theory', in E. Le Jallé and A. Benoit (eds) *Thinking with Women Philosophers: Critical Essays in Practical Contemporary Philosophy*, Cham: Springer International Publishing, pp 75–103.

Lemus, D., Farruggia, S.P., Germo, G., and Chang, E.S. (2017) 'The plans, goals, and concerns of pre-emancipated youth in foster care', *Children and Youth Services Review*, 78: 48–55.

Lister, R. (2021) *Poverty* (2nd edn), Cambridge: Polity Press.

Lock, A. and Strong, T. (2010) *Social Constructionism: Sources and Stirrings in Theory and Practice*, Cambridge: Cambridge University Press.

Lushey, C.J. and Munro, E.R. (2015) 'Participatory peer research methodology: an effective method for obtaining young people's perspectives on transitions from care to adulthood?', *Qualitative Social Work*, 14(4): 522–537.

Lynch, A., Alderson, H., Kerridge, G., Johnson, R., McGovern, R., Newlands, F., et al (2021) 'An inter-disciplinary perspective on evaluation of innovation to support care leavers' transition', *Journal of Children's Services*, 16(3): 214–232.

Masterson, D., Areskoug Josefsson, K., Robert, G., Nylander, E., and Kjellström, S. (2022) 'Mapping definitions of co-production and co-design in health and social care: a systematic scoping review providing lessons for the future', *Health Expectations*, 25(3): 902–913.

Matchett, E., and Appleton, P. (2023) ' "I make a lot of the choices myself – I think I've taught myself that through the imbalance of support": the internal conversations, reflexivity, and post-school educational achievement of care-experienced young people', *British Educational Research Journal*, https://doi.org/10.1002/berj.3906.

Maxwell, K., Awatere, S., Ratana, K., Davies, K., and Taiapa, C. (2020) 'He waka eke noa/we are all in the same boat: a framework for co-governance from Aotearoa New Zealand', *Marine Policy*, 121: 104213.

McCabe, E., Amarbayan, M., Rabi, S., Mendoza, J., Naqvi, S.F., Thapa Bajgain, K., et al (2023) 'Youth engagement in mental health research: a systematic review', *Health Expectations*, 26(1): 30–50.

McCrory, E., Foulkes, L., and Viding, E. (2022) 'Social thinning and stress generation after childhood maltreatment: a neurocognitive social transactional model of psychiatric vulnerability', *The Lancet Psychiatry*, 9(10): 828–837.

McDowall, J.J. (2016) 'Connection to culture by indigenous children and young people in out-of-home care in Australia', *Communities, Children and Families Australia*, 10(1): 5–26.

McTavish, J.R., McKee, C. and MacMillan, H.L. (2022) 'Foster children's perspectives on participation in child welfare processes: a meta-synthesis of qualitative studies', *PLOS One*, 17(10): e0275784.

Mendes, P., and Moslehuddin, B. (2006) 'From dependence to interdependence: towards better outcomes for young people leaving state care', *Child Abuse Review: Journal of the British Association for the Study and Prevention of Child Abuse and Neglect*, 15(2): 110–126.

Mendes, P., and Rogers, J. (2020) 'Young people transitioning from out-of-home care: what are the lessons from extended care programmes in the USA and England for Australia?', *The British Journal of Social Work*, 50(5): 1513–1530.

Mendes, P. and Snow, P. (eds) (2016) *Young People Transitioning from Out-Of-Home Care: International Research, Policy and Practice*, Cham: Springer.

Mendes, P., Johnson, G., and Moslehuddin, B. (2012) 'Young people transitioning from out-of-home care and relationships with family of origin: an examination of three recent Australian studies', *Child Care in Practice*, 18(4): 357–370.

Mendes, P., Martin, R., Jau, M.J., and Chavulak, M.J. (2023) 'An analysis of the intersecting factors and needs that informed the experiences of young people transitioning from out of home care in the Australian states of Victoria and Western Australia', *Children and Youth Services Review*, 149: 106949.

Mendes, P., Purtell, J., Morris, S., Berger, E., Baidawi, S., D'Souza, L., et al (2023) 'Examining the role of lived experience consultants in an Australian research study on the educational experiences of children and young people in out-of-home care', *Qualitative Social Work*, 22(5): 975–991.

Mendes, P., Purtell, J., and Waugh, J. (2022) 'Advancing the social rights of care leavers: towards a new community-based social network and peer support modle for supporting young people transitioning from out of home care in times of crisis', *New Community (Australia)*, 78: 58–62.

Mendes, P., Standfield, R., Saunders, B., McCurdy, S., Walsh, J., and Turnbull, L. (2021) 'Aboriginal and Torres Strait Islander (Indigenous) young people leaving out-of-home care in Australia: a national scoping study', *Children and Youth Services Review*, 121: 105848.

Merleau-Ponty, M. (1962) *Phenomenology of Perception*, translated from the French by Colin Smith, London: Routledge and Kegan Paul.

Miles, S.R., Martindale, S.L., Flanagan, J.C., Troyanskaya, M., Reljic, T., Gilmore, A.K., et al (2023) 'Putting the pieces together to understand anger in combat veterans and service members: psychological and physical contributors', *Journal of Psychiatric Research*, 159: 57–65.

Millgram, E. (2014) 'Segmented agency', in M. Vargas and G. Yaffe (eds) *Rational and Social Agency: The Philosophy of Michael Bratman*, Oxford: Oxford University Press, pp 152–189.

Millgram, E. (2019) 'Bounded agency', in L. Ferrero (ed.) *The Routledge Handbook of Philosophy of Agency*, Abingdon: Routledge, pp 68–76.

Morton, J.M. (2011) 'Toward an ecological theory of the norms of practical deliberation', *European Journal of Philosophy*, 19(4): 561–584.

Moss, M.P. (2010) 'American Indian health disparities: by the sufferance of Congress', *Hamline Journal of Public Law and Policy*, 32: 59–82.

Munford, R. and Sanders, J. (2015) 'Young people's search for agency: making sense of their experiences and taking control', *Qualitative Social Work*, 14(5): 616–633.

Munford, R., and Sanders, J. (2020) 'Shame and recognition: social work practice with vulnerable young people', *Child & Family Social Work*, 25(1): 53–61.

Munro, E.R. (2019) 'Reflections on upholding the rights of youth leaving out-of-home care', in V.R. Mann-Feder and M. Goyette (eds) *Leaving Care and the Transition to Adulthood: International Contributions to Theory, Research, and Practice,* Oxford: Oxford University Press, pp 69–86.

Munro, E.R., Pinkerton, J., Mendes, P., Hyde-Dryden, G., Herczog, M., and Benbenishty, R. (2011) 'The contribution of the United Nations Convention on the Rights of the Child to understanding and promoting the interests of young people making the transition from care to adulthood', *Children and Youth Services Review*, 33(12): 2417–2423.

Murray, E.T., Lacey, R., Maughan, B., and Sacker, A. (2020) 'Association of childhood out-of-home care status with all-cause mortality up to 42-years later: Office of National Statistics Longitudinal Study', *BMC Public Health*, 20(1): 1–10.

Murrup-Stewart, C., Whyman, T., Jobson, L., and Adams, K. (2021) ' "Connection to culture is like a massive lifeline": yarning with aboriginal young people about culture and social and emotional wellbeing', *Qualitative Health Research*, 31(10): 1833–1846.

Naylor, P.B., Petch, L., Ali, P.A., Monks, C.P., and Coyne, I. (2011) 'Domestic violence: bullying in the home', in C.P. Monks and I. Coyne (eds) *Bullying in Different Contexts*, Cambridge: Cambridge University Press, pp 87–112.

Ndlovu-Gatsheni, S. (2018) *Epistemic Freedom in Africa: Deprovincialization and Decolonization,* London: Routledge.

Nikulina, V., and Widom, C.S. (2013) 'Child maltreatment and executive functioning in middle adulthood: a prospective examination', *Neuropsychology*, 27(4): 417–427.

Nussbaum, M.C. (2001) *Upheavals of Thought: The Intelligence of Emotions,* Cambridge: Cambridge University Press.

O'Donnell, M., Taplin, S., Marriott, R., Lima, F., and Stanley, F.J. (2019) 'Infant removals: the need to address the over-representation of Aboriginal infants and community concerns of another "stolen generation"', *Child Abuse & Neglect*, 90: 88–98.

Ogden, T.H. (1997) 'Listening three Frost poems', *Psychoanalytic Dialogues*, 7(5): 619–639.

Ogrizek, A., Radjack, R., Moro, M.R., and Lachal, J. (2022) 'The cultural hybridization of mothering in French prison nurseries: a qualitative study', *Culture, Medicine, and Psychiatry*, 47(2): 422–442.

Okpych, N. (2012) 'Policy framework supporting youth aging-out of foster care through college: review and recommendations', *Children and Youth Services Review*, 34(7): 1390–1396.

Okpych, N.J. and Courtney, M.E. (2017) 'Who goes to college? Social capital and other predictors of college enrollment for foster-care youth', *Journal of the Society for Social Work and Research*, 8(4): 563–593.

Okpych, N.J., Park, S., Powers, J., Harty, J.S., and Courtney, M.E. (2023) 'Relationships that persist and protect: the role of enduring relationships on early-adult outcomes among youth transitioning out of foster care', *Social Service Review*, 97(4), doi: https://doi.org/10.1086/724736

Orlove, B., Dawson, N., Sherpa, P., Adelekan, I., Alangui, W., Carmona, R., et al (2022) *ICSM CHC White Paper I: Intangible Cultural Heritage, Diverse Knowledge Systems and Climate Change. Contribution of Knowledge Systems Group I to the International Co-Sponsored Meeting on Culture, Heritage and Climate Change.* Discussion Paper. ICOMOS &ISCM CHC, Charenton-le-Pont, France.

Oshri, A., Duprey, E.B., Kogan, S.M., Carlson, M.W. and Liu, S. (2018) 'Growth patterns of future orientation among maltreated youth: a prospective examination of the emergence of resilience', *Developmental Psychology*, 54(8): 1456–1471.

Packer, M.J. (2018) *The Science of Qualitative Research* (2nd edn), Cambridge: Cambridge University Press.

Park, K., and Courtney, M.E. (2022) 'Mitigating risks of incarceration among transition-age foster youth: considering domains of social bonds', *Child and Adolescent Social Work Journal*, 40: 473–486.

Park, S.E., Powers, J., Okpych, N.J., and Courtney, M.E. (2020) 'Predictors of foster youths' participation in their transitional independent living plan (TILP) development: calling for collaborative case plan decision-making processes', *Children and Youth Services Review*, 115: 105051.

Park, S., Powers, J., Okpych, N.J., and Courtney, M.E. (2022) 'Co-production of care leavers' transition planning as young adults: an analysis of young people in California foster care', *The British Journal of Social Work*, 52(6): 3385–3405.

Patterson, A.S., Kuperus, T., and Hershey, M. (2023) *Africa's Urban Youth: Challenging Marginalization, Claiming Citizenship*, Cambridge: Cambridge University Press.

Paulsen, V., and Thomas, N. (2018) 'The transition to adulthood from care as a struggle for recognition', *Child & Family Social Work*, 23(2): 163–170.

Peguero, A.A., and Hong, J.S. (2020) *School Bullying: Youth Vulnerability, Marginalization, and Victimization*, Cham: Springer Nature Switzerland.

Provost, M., and Crary, A. (2022) 'Wittgenstein and feminism: Alice Crary in conversation with Mickaëlle Provost', *Nordic Wittgenstein Review* (special issue).

Pryce, J., Napolitano, L., and Samuels, G.M. (2017) 'Transition to adulthood of former foster youth: multilevel challenges to the help-seeking process', *Emerging Adulthood*, 5(5): 311–321.

Purvis, B., Mao, Y., and Robinson, D. (2019) 'Three pillars of sustainability: in search of conceptual origins', *Sustainability Science*, 14: 681–695.

Ratcliffe, M. (2019) 'Emotional intentionality', *Royal Institute of Philosophy Supplement*, 85: 251–269.

Ratcliffe, M., Ruddell, M. and Smith, B. (2014) 'What is a "sense of foreshortened future?" A phenomenological study of trauma, trust, and time', *Frontiers in Psychology*, 5: Article 1026.

Raza, S. (2022) 'Max Weber and Charles Taylor: on normative aspects of a theory of human action', *Journal of Classical Sociology*, 23(1): 97–136. doi:1468795X221080770.

Read, R. (2018) 'Can there be a logic of grief?: Why Wittgenstein and Merleau-Ponty say "yes"', in O. Kuusela, M. Ometita and T. Uçan (eds) *Wittgenstein and Phenomenology*, London: Routledge, pp 176–196.

Read, R. (2020) *Wittgenstein's Liberatory Philosophy: Thinking Through His Philosophical Investigations,* London: Routledge.

Refaeli, T., Benbenishty, R., and Zeira, A. (2019) 'Predictors of life satisfaction among care leavers: a mixed-method longitudinal study', *Children and Youth Services Review*, 99: 146–155.

Refaeli, T., Shuman-Harel, N., Brady, E., Mann-Feder, V., Munro, E., and van Breda, A.D. (2023) 'Widening the care gap? An international comparison of care-leaving in the time of COVID-19', *American Journal of Orthopsychiatry*, 93(5): 436–449.

Riebschleger, J., Day, A., and Damashek, A. (2015) 'Foster care youth share stories of trauma before, during, and after placement: youth voices for building trauma-informed systems of care', *Journal of Aggression, Maltreatment & Trauma*, 24(4): 339–360.

Rios, S.J. and Rocco, T.S. (2014) 'From foster care to college: barriers and supports on the road to postsecondary education', *Emerging Adulthood*, 2(3): 227–237.

Ritunnano, R., Papola, D., Broome, M.R., and Nelson, B. (2023) 'Phenomenology as a resource for translational research in mental health: methodological trends, challenges and new directions', *Epidemiology and Psychiatric Sciences*, 32: e5.

Roche, P., Shimmin, C., Hickes, S., Khan, M., Sherzoi, O., Wicklund, E., et al (2020) 'Valuing all voices: refining a trauma-informed, intersectional and critical reflexive framework for patient engagement in health research using a qualitative descriptive approach', *Research Involvement and Engagement*, 6(1): 1–13.

Sacker, A., Lacey, R.E., Maughan, B., and Murray, E.T. (2022) 'Out-of-home care in childhood and socio-economic functioning in adulthood: ONS longitudinal study 1971–2011', *Children and Youth Services Review*, 132: 106300.

Sacker, A., Murray, E., Lacey, R., and Maughan, B. (2021) 'The lifelong health and wellbeing trajectories of people who have been in care: findings from the Looked-after Children Grown up Project', Nuffield Foundation.

Salami, B., Denga, B., Taylor, R., Ajayi, N., Jackson, M., Asefaw, M., and Salma, J. (2021) 'Original qualitative research: access to mental health for Black youths in Alberta', *Health Promotion and Chronic Disease Prevention in Canada: Research, Policy and Practice*, 41(9): 245.

Salmon, S., Garces Davila, I., Taillieu, T.L., Stewart-Tufescu, A., Duncan, L., Fortier, J., et al (2022) 'Adolescent health outcomes: associations with child maltreatment and peer victimization', *BMC Public Health*, 22(1): 1–13.

Samuels, E. (2017) 'Six ways of looking at crip time', *Disability Studies Quarterly*, 37(3), doi: https://doi.org/10.18061/dsq. v37i3.5824

Samuels, G.M. and Pryce, J.M. (2008) ' "What doesn't kill you makes you stronger": survivalist self-reliance as resilience and risk among young adults aging out of foster care', *Children and Youth Services Review*, 30(10): 1198–1210.

Schäfer, M., Korn, S., Smith, P.K., Hunter, S.C., Mora-Merchán, J.A., Singer, M.M., and Van der Meulen, K. (2004) 'Lonely in the crowd: recollections of bullying', *British Journal of Developmental Psychology*, 22(3): 379–394.

Schelbe, L. (2023) *Some Type of Way: Aging Out of Foster Care*, Oxford: Oxford University Press.

Schofield, G., Larsson, B. and Ward, E. (2017) 'Risk, resilience and identity construction in the life narratives of young people leaving residential care', *Child & Family Social Work*, 22(2): 782–791.

Schoon, I., and Heckhausen, J. (2019) 'Conceptualizing individual agency in the transition from school to work: a social-ecological developmental perspective', *Adolescent Research Review*, 4(2): 135–148.

Schoon, I., and Lyons-Amos, M. (2017) 'A socio-ecological model of agency: the role of structure and agency in shaping education and employment transitions in England', *Journal of Longitudinal and Lifecourse Studies*, 8(1): 35–56.

Seker, S., Boonmann, C., Gerger, H., Jäggi, L., d'Huart, D., Schmeck, K., and Schmid, M. (2022) 'Mental disorders among adults formerly in out-of-home care: a systematic review and meta-analysis of longitudinal studies', *European Child & Adolescent Psychiatry*, 31(12): 1963–1982.

Sekibo, B. (2020) 'Experiences of young people early in the transition from residential care in Lagos State, Nigeria', *Emerging Adulthood*, 8(1): 92–100.

Shah, M.F., Liu, Q., Mark Eddy, J., Barkan, S., Marshall, D., Mancuso, D., et al (2017) 'Predicting homelessness among emerging adults aging out of foster care', *American Journal of Community Psychology*, 60(1–2): 33–43.

Sharpe, D., Rajabi, M., Harden, A., Moodambail, A.R., and Hakeem, V. (2021) 'Supporting disengaged children and young people living with diabetes to self-care: a qualitative study in a socially disadvantaged and ethnically diverse urban area', *BMJ Open*, 11(10): e046989.

Shimmin, C., Wittmeier, K.D., Lavoie, J.G., Wicklund, E.D., and Sibley, K.M. (2017) 'Moving towards a more inclusive patient and public involvement in health research paradigm: the incorporation of a trauma-informed intersectional analysis', *BMC Health Services Research*, 17: 1–10.

Shulman, S., and Nurmi, J.E. (2010) 'Understanding emerging adulthood from a goalsetting perspective', in S. Shulman and J.-E. Nurmi (eds) *The Role of Goals in Navigating Individual Lives during Emerging Adulthood. New Directions for Child and Adolescent Development,* 130(special issue): 1–11.

Silove, D., Brooks, R., Steel, C.R.B., Steel, Z., Hewage, K., Rodger, J., and Soosay, I. (2009) 'Explosive anger as a response to human rights violations in post-conflict Timor-Leste', *Social Science & Medicine*, 69(5): 670–677.

Simpson, A. (2017) 'The ruse of consent and the anatomy of 'refusal': cases from indigenous North America and Australia', *Postcolonial Studies*, 20(1): 18–33.

Simpson, N.P., Clarke, J., Orr, S.A., Cundill, G., Orlove, B., Fatorić, S., et al (2022) 'Decolonizing climate change–heritage research', *Nature Climate Change*, 12(3): 210–213.

Sissay, L. (2019) *My Name Is Why: A Memoir,* Edinburgh: Canongate.

Sluga, H. (2011) *Wittgenstein,* Chichester: Wiley-Blackwell.

Smith, J.A. (2019) 'Participants and researchers searching for meaning: conceptual developments for interpretative phenomenological analysis', *Qualitative Research in Psychology*, 16(2): 166–181.

Smith, J.A., and Nizza, I.E. (2022) *Essentials of Interpretative Phenomenological Analysis*, Washington, DC: American Psychological Association.

Smith, J.A., Flowers, P., and Larkin, M. (2009) *Interpretative Phenomenological Analysis: Theory, Method and Research*, London: Sage Publications.

Smith, J.M., and Alloy, L.B. (2009) 'A roadmap to rumination: a review of the definition, assessment, and conceptualization of this multifaceted construct', *Clinical Psychology Review*, 29(2): 116–128.

Spencer, F.S. (2014) 'Why did the "Leper" get under Jesus' skin? Emotion theory and angry reaction in Mark 1: 40–45', *Horizons in Biblical Theology*, 36(2): 107–128.

Srivastava, P., and Hopwood, N. (2009) 'A practical iterative framework for qualitative data analysis', *International Journal of Qualitative Methods*, 8(1): 76–84.

Srivastava, P., and Hopwood, N. (2018) 'Reflection/commentary on a past article: "A practical iterative framework for qualitative data analysis"', *International Journal of Qualitative Methods*, 17(1): 1–3.

St John, N., and Akama, Y. (2022) 'Reimagining co-design on Country as a relational and transformational practice', *CoDesign*, 18(1): 16–31.

Stein, M. (2006) 'Young people aging out of care: the poverty of theory', *Children and Youth Services Review*, 28(4): 422–434.

Stein, M. (2012) *Young People Leaving Care: Supporting Pathways to Adulthood*, London: Jessica Kingsley Publishers.

Stein, M. (2021) 'The rights movement of young people living in and leaving care in England between 1973 and 2011: a history from below', *Child & Family Social Work*, 26(2): 280–287.

Steinbeck, P. (2017) *Message to Our Folks: The Art Ensemble of Chicago*, Chicago: Chicago University Press.

Steine, I.M., Winje, D., Krystal, J.H., Bjorvatn, B., Milde, A.M., Grønli, J., et al (2017) 'Cumulative childhood maltreatment and its dose-response relation with adult symptomatology: findings in a sample of adult survivors of sexual abuse', *Child Abuse & Neglect*, 65: 99–111.

Stern, D. (1991) 'The "Middle Wittgenstein": from logical atomism to practical holism', *Synthese*, 87(2): 203–226.

Stewart, Dawn L. (2016) 'Fragmented lives: a qualitative study of the experiences of Black youth who have aged out of the foster care system', PhD in Educational Studies, Eastern Michigan University, Ypsilanti, MI.

Storm, M., and Edwards, A. (2013) 'Models of user involvement in the mental health context: intentions and implementation challenges', *Psychiatric Quarterly*, 84(3): 313–327.

Storø, J. (2017) 'Which transition concept is useful for describing the process of young people leaving state care? A reflection on research and language', *European Journal of Social Work*, 20(5): 770–781.

Strahl, B., van Breda, A.D.P., Mann-Feder, V., and Schröer, W. (2020) 'A multinational comparison of care-leaving policy and legislation', *Journal of International and Comparative Social Policy*, 37(1): 1–16.

Stubbs, A., Baidawi, S., and Mendes, P. (2022) 'Young people transitioning from out-of-home care: their experience of informal support. A scoping review', *Children and Youth Services Review*, 144: 106735.

Suddendorf, T. and Busby, J. (2005) 'Making decisions with the future in mind: developmental and comparative identification of mental time travel', *Learning and Motivation*, 36(2): 110–125.

Suddendorf, T., Addis, D.R., and Corballis, M.C. (2009) 'Mental time travel and the shaping of the human mind', *Philosophical Transactions of the Royal Society B: Biological Sciences*, 364(1521): 1317–1324.

Sulimani-Aidan, Y. (2015) 'Do they get what they expect?: The connection between young adults' future expectations before leaving care and outcomes after leaving care', *Children and Youth Services Review*, 55: 193–200.

Sweeney, A., Filson, B., Kennedy, A., Collinson, L., and Gillard, S. (2018) 'A paradigm shift: relationships in trauma-informed mental health services', *BJPsych Advances*, 24(5): 319–333.

Szanto, T., Meindl, P., and Zahavi, D. (2023) 'Introduction: Husserl and community', *Continental Philosophy Review*, 56: 335–341.

Tarrow, S. (2010) 'The strategy of paired comparison: toward a theory of practice', *Comparative Political Studies*, 43(2): 230–259.

Taussig, H.N. and Raviv, T. (2022) 'Foster care and child well-being', in R.D. Krugman and J.E. Korbin (eds) *Handbook of Child Maltreatment*, Cham: Springer.

Taylor, C. (1985) *Human Agency and Language: Philosophical Papers 1*, Cambridge: Cambridge University Press.

Taylor, C. (1994) 'The politics of recognition', in A. Gutmann (ed.) *Multiculturalism: Examining the Politics of Recognition*, Princeton, NJ: Princeton University Press, pp 25–73.

Taylor, C. (2016) *The Language Animal: The Full Shape of the Human Linguistic Capacity,* Cambridge, MA, and London: The Belknap Press of Harvard University Press.

Taylor, D., Albers, B., Mann, G., Chakraborty, S. Lewis, J. Mendes, P., et al (2021) 'Systematic review and meta-analysis of policies, programmes and interventions that improve outcomes for young people leaving the out-of-home care system', London: What Works for Children's Social Care.

Teicher, M.H., Gordon, J.B., and Nemeroff, C.B. (2022) 'Recognizing the importance of childhood maltreatment as a critical factor in psychiatric diagnoses, treatment, research, prevention, and education', *Molecular Psychiatry*, 27(3): 1331–1338.

Theron, L., and van Breda, A. (2021) 'Multisystemic enablers of sub-Saharan child and youth resilience to maltreatment', *Child Abuse & Neglect*, 119: 105083.

Törrönen, M.L., and Vornanen, R.H. (2014) 'Young people leaving care: participatory research to improve child welfare practices and the rights of children and young people', *Australian Social Work*, 67(1): 135–150.

Trocmé, N., Doucet, M., Fallon, B., Nutton, J., and Esposito, T. (2023) 'Child welfare in Canada', in J.D. Berrick, N. Gilbert and M. Skivenes (eds) *The Oxford Handbook of Child Protection Systems*, Oxford: Oxford University Press, pp 90–111.

Tuval-Mashiach, R. (2017) 'Raising the curtain: the importance of transparency in qualitative research', *Qualitative Psychology*, 4(2): 126.

Unrau, Y.A., Seita, J.R. and Putney, K.S. (2008) 'Former foster youth remember multiple placement moves: a journey of loss and hope', *Children and Youth Services Review*, 30(11): 1256–1266.

van Breda, A.D.P., and Frimpong-Manso, K. (2020) 'Leaving care in Africa', *Emerging Adulthood*, 8(1): 3–5.

van Breda, A.D., Munro, E.R., Gilligan, R., Anghel, R., Harder, A., Incarnato, M., et al (2020) 'Extended care: global dialogue on policy, practice and research', *Children and Youth Services Review*, 119: 105596.

van Breda, A.D.P., and Pinkerton, J. (2020) 'Raising African voices in the global dialogue on care-leaving and emerging adulthood', *Emerging Adulthood*, 8(1): 6–15.

van Breda, A.D. (2022) 'The contribution of supportive relationships to care-leaving outcomes: a longitudinal resilience study in South Africa', *Child Care in Practice*, 1–16.

Van der Kolk, B. (2014) *The Body Keeps the Score: Mind, Brain and Body in the Transformation of Trauma*, London: Penguin.

Vandenberghe, F. (2005) 'Book review: *The Archers*: a tale of folk (final episode?)', *European Journal of Social Theory*, 8(2): 227–237.

Vandenberghe, F. (2022) 'Critical realist hermeneutics', *Journal of Critical Realism*, 21(5): 552–570.

Vasileiou, K., Barnett, J., Thorpe, S., and Young, T. (2018) 'Characterising and justifying sample size sufficiency in interview-based studies: systematic analysis of qualitative health research over a 15-year period', *BMC Medical Research Methodology*, 18(1): 1–18.

Victorian Department of Justice (2013) 'Victorian Aboriginal Justice Agreement: Phase 3. A partnership between the Victorian government and Koori community', Retrieved from http:// www.justice.vic.gov.au

Viksveen, P., Cardenas, N.E., Ibenfeldt, M., Meldahl, L.G., Krijger, L., Game, J.R., et al (2022) 'Involvement of adolescent representatives and coresearchers in mental health research: experiences from a research project', *Health Expectations*, 25(1): 322–332.

Wade, J. (2008) 'The ties that bind: support from birth families and substitute families for young people leaving care', *British Journal of Social Work*, 38(1): 39–54.

Wang, S., Walsh, K., and Li, J. (2023) 'A prospective longitudinal study of multidomain resilience among youths with and without maltreatment histories', *Development and Psychopathology*, February: 1–15. doi:10.1017/S0954579423000032.

Wasson, S. (2021) 'Waiting, strange: transplant recipient experience, medical time and queer/crip temporalities', *Medical Humanities*, 47(4): 447–455.

Weegels, J., Jefferson, A.M., and Martin, T.M. (2020) 'Introduction: confinement beyond site: connecting urban and prison ethnographies', *The Cambridge Journal of Anthropology*, 38(1): 1–14.

West-Newman, C.L. (2004) 'Anger in legacies of empire: Indigenous peoples and settler states', *European Journal of Social Theory*, 7(2): 189–208.

Wiemann, A.K., Werner, A., Konrad, K., Niestroj, S.C., Steden, S., and Lohaus, A. (2023) 'Lifetime poly-victimization and later bullying victimization: associations with internalizing problems and out-of-home care', *Child Abuse & Neglect*, 135: 105970.

Williams, Daniel C. and Levitt, Heidi M. (2007) 'Principles for facilitating agency in psychotherapy', *Psychotherapy Research*, 17(1): 66–82.

Wimalasena, L. (2022) 'Critical realism, reflexivity and the missing voice of the subaltern: the case of postcolonial Sri Lanka', in N. Jammulamadaka and S. Ul-Haq (eds) *Managing the Post-Colony South Asia Focus*, Singapore: Springer, pp 101–120.

Wittgenstein, L. (1958, 1969) *The Blue and Brown Books: Preliminary Studies for the 'Philosophical Investigations'*, Oxford: Blackwell.

Wittgenstein, L. (2009 [1953]) *Philosophical Investigations* (revised 4th edn), Chichester: Wiley-Blackwell.

Wojciak, A.S., Tomfohrde, O., Simpson, J.E., and Waid, J. (2023) 'Sibling separation: learning from those with former foster care experiences', *The British Journal of Social Work*, 53(4): 2198–2216.

Wright, M., Brown, A., Dudgeon, P., McPhee, R., Coffin, J., Pearson, G., et al (2021) 'Our journey, our story: a study protocol for the evaluation of a co-design framework to improve services for Aboriginal youth mental health and well-being', *BMJ Open*, 11(5): e042981.

Yi, Y., Edwards, F.R., and Wildeman, C. (2020) 'Cumulative prevalence of confirmed maltreatment and foster care placement for US children by race/ethnicity, 2011–2016', *American Journal of Public Health*, 110(5): 704–709.

Yoshioka-Maxwell, A. (2022) 'Experiences of abuse: homeless former foster youth and their experiences of abuse in out-of-home care', *Child and Adolescent Social Work Journal*, 40(3): 1–10.

Zaragocin, S., and Caretta, M.A. (2021) 'Cuerpo-territorio: a decolonial feminist geographical method for the study of embodiment', *Annals of the American Association of Geographers*, 111(5): 1503–1518.

Zimmermann, J. (2015) *Hermeneutics: A Very Short Introduction*, Oxford: Oxford University Press.

Zolkos, M. (2019) 'The "endangered voices" of the Taiwanese victims of Japanese sexual slavery', *Public Philosophy Journal*, 2(2): 1–10.

Index

References to endnotes show both the page number
and the note number (231n3).

What Matters and Who Matters

see also interpretative
 phenomenological analysis (IPA)
imagination 77–78
importance (what and who matters)
 see what and who matters
In a Different Voice (Gilligan) 119, 136
Indigenous knowledge
 systems 125–126
Indigenous young people 18,
 124, 142n30
internal conversations
 about 3, 17
 examples of 45, 107
 mental health and 46
 and reflexivity 20, 76–78
 research interview framework
 12–14, 37, 38
 research participants on 5, 12, 15,
 20, 46, 48, 57, 64, 67, 68, 80,
 146n4 (chap 3)
 self-reflections on 30
interpretative phenomenological
 analysis (IPA)
 about 25–26
 idiography 25, 36, 37–38, 85,
 143n62, 144n36
 transcripts, (re-)reading of 5, 22,
 35, 37, 62, 76, 86, 88
 transparency 36
 see also research
interviews see internal conversations;
 research interviews; transcripts
IPA see interpretative
 phenomenological analysis (IPA)

J

Joe (research participant)
 about 74, 76
 on education 77
 on friends 77, 79
 on future planning 78, 80–81
 personal logic of 86, 104
 on what and who matters 76–77,
 79, 85

K

Kafer, Alison 139n6
kinship care 19
Kulmala, Meri 143n55

L

language
 approaches to 39–40

attention to, paying 104
expressive 136
The Language Animal (Taylor) 39
Lebensform (form of life) 103, 106
Letter to Readers (Gilligan) 119
logic
 counterlogic 101, 102, 104, 120, 136
 as embedded in life 105
 as expressive voice 106–107
 and facial features 105–106
 as fluid 103–105
 of grief 105, 113, 115–117
 as not synoptic (an overview) 108
 personal logic of participants 38,
 42, 46, 47, 51, 85–86,
 102–103, 104

M

Making Our Way through the World
 (Archer) 16
maltreatment 18, 32, 141n23
Māori 125–126, 128–129
memory
 and future planning 33
 as object of emotion 111–112
Mendes, Philip 17–18
mental health 3, 18, 46
mental time travel
 about 33–34
 and future planning 85, 90, 96, 98
 research participants' use of 49, 50,
 52, 55, 59, 60, 84
 see also reflexivity; sense of personal
 time; time
Merleau-Ponty, Maurice 31
methodological sensitivities for
 co-producing knowledge
 through enduring trustful
 partnerships 128–129, 132,
 133, 136–137
Millgram, Elijah 98–99, 104
Morton, Jennifer 99, 104
Moslehuddin, Badal 17–18
multifaceted reflexivity 34, 35, 43,
 44, 76, 90
Munro, Emily R. 130

N

Nailah (research participant)
 about 63
 on education 64, 69, 72–73
 emotions experienced by
 109–110, 112

Printed in the USA
CPSIA information can be obtained
at www.ICGtesting.com
JSHW011546160324
J9318JS00004B/63

9 781447 368335